Contents

AF866545

Introduction

Imagine the day you finally pull the trigger on early retirement. You have run the spreadsheets a hundred times. Your withdrawal rate is a conservative three point five percent. Your asset allocation is bulletproof, stress-tested against historical crashes, inflation spikes, and bear markets. You walk out of your workplace for the last time, leaving behind the fluorescent lights and the endless Zoom calls, armed with a master plan for the next chapter of your life.

Then, a few weeks later, you sit down at your kitchen table to buy health insurance.

You log onto the government exchange, enter your age, and pull up the monthly premiums for a standard, middle-of-the-road health plan for a couple in their late fifties. The number staring back at you makes your chest tighten. It is not a bill; it is a second mortgage. It is twelve, fifteen, maybe even twenty thousand dollars a year in premiums alone, with an out-of-pocket maximum that could require another fifteen thousand if someone actually gets sick.

Suddenly, your pristine financial plan begins to crack. To pay for this exorbitant health insurance, you realize you will need to withdraw more money from your tax-deferred retirement accounts. But pulling more money out of those accounts increases your taxable income. And here is the cruelest joke of all: because Affordable Care Act subsidies are tied directly to your income, generating that extra cash just disqualified you from the financial assistance that would have made the insurance affordable in the first place.

You haven't just encountered an expense. You have stepped into the tax-healthcare doom loop.

For decades, the single greatest barrier to retiring before age 65 wasn't a lack of savings; it was the terrifying prospect of losing employer-sponsored health insurance. Before 2014, if you had a pre-existing condition—which the insurance industry previously defined as anything from a prior heart attack to a history of asthma—buying a private policy on the open market was either prohibitively expensive or mathematically impossible. You were bound to your desk by the golden handcuffs of corporate benefits, forced to wait out the clock until Medicare kicked in at age 65.

The Affordable Care Act changed the fundamental physics of early retirement. By making it illegal to deny coverage or charge higher premiums based on medical history, the law blew the doors off the traditional retirement timeline. But in solving the underwriting problem, the system introduced a remarkably complex financial puzzle. It replaced a medical underwriting system with an income underwriting system.

If you are going to retire early, you have to understand a deeply counterintuitive reality: in the world of modern health insurance, your net worth is entirely irrelevant. The Marketplace does not care if you have five million dollars sitting in a brokerage account, a paid-off house, and a yacht parked in the marina. It only cares about a very specific, highly manipulable number on your tax return called MAGI—Modified Adjusted Gross Income.

Because subsidies are tied exclusively to MAGI, two early retirees living in the same zip code can have wildly different experiences. One is a multimillionaire who carefully structures their cash flow to show forty thousand dollars of taxable income. They receive massive government subsidies, unlocking a gold-tier health plan for pennies on the dollar. The other is a frugal middle-class saver who unthinkingly cashes out an eighty-thousand-dollar pension or carelessly sells a highly appreciated mutual fund in the wrong calendar year. They are immediately flagged as "high income" by the exchange algorithms, stripped of their subsidies, and left to pay the full, brutal retail price for their coverage.

The difference between these two retirees isn't luck. It isn't even wealth. The difference is income engineering.

Most intelligent people approach health insurance the same way they approach car insurance. They assume it is a static product you shop for once a year, comparing deductibles and premiums in a vacuum to find the best deal. But during the "gap years"—that critical window of time between your final paycheck and your sixty-fifth birthday—health insurance is not a line item in your budget. It is a dynamic, living tax bracket. Every dollar you spend, and more importantly, *where* you source that dollar, dictates what you will pay for medical care.

If you understand the rules of this system, you can legally and ethically bend the math in your favor. If you ignore the rules, you will bleed capital at a rate that can threaten your long-term financial independence.

The goal ahead of us is to completely rewire how you think about paying for your life between today and Medicare. You are going to learn how to view your healthcare costs and your tax strategy as one integrated machine. You will stop asking, "Which health plan is the cheapest?" and start asking, "How can I source my living expenses this year to trigger the exact level of subsidy I want?"

To do this, we have to pull back the curtain on how the Affordable Care Act actually calculates your worth. We will dissect the mechanics of advance premium tax credits, breaking down the strange, interconnected relationship between the "benchmark" silver plans in your county and the percentage of the federal poverty level you happen to fall into. You will learn why a Silver plan is sometimes vastly superior to a Gold plan, not because of the premium, but because of hidden, income-based cost-sharing reductions that magically lower your deductibles and copays—provided you land your income in the exact right sweet spot.

But understanding the insurance rules is only half the battle. The real magic happens when we connect those rules to your investment portfolio.

You are going to learn the dark art of MAGI management. We will look at your assets not just as pools of money, but as levers you can pull to manipulate your tax return. We will explore how to sequence your withdrawals across taxable brokerages, tax-deferred IRAs, Roth accounts, and cash reserves. You will discover how a well-timed Roth conversion can be a brilliant tax move in your seventies, but a catastrophic mistake at age fifty-nine if it accidentally pushes you over a subsidy threshold. You will see how capital gains, part-time consulting income, and even the interest on your bank accounts all conspire to inflate your MAGI, and how you can use tools like Health Savings Accounts and strategic deductions to artificially suppress it.

This isn't about evading the system; it is about playing the board game exactly as it was designed. The government has published the rulebook. The math is hiding in plain sight. It is entirely up to you to arrange your affairs to optimize the outcome.

Of course, a brilliant tax strategy is useless if your health plan doesn't actually let you see your doctor. The gap years are not a theoretical exercise in tax avoidance; they are a time when human bodies predictably begin to require more maintenance. Therefore, we will also focus heavily on the gritty, practical reality of using these plans. You will learn how to interrogate a plan's network, ensuring your preferred specialists and necessary prescription drugs are actually covered before you lock yourself into a twelve-month contract. We will build a framework for choosing between the Marketplace, keeping your former employer's coverage through COBRA, or leaning on a spouse's plan, weighing the hidden costs and benefits of each path.

More importantly, you will learn how to defend your plan against the chaos of real life. Early retirement is rarely a static period. Markets crash, forcing you to change your withdrawal strategy. You might decide to pick up some freelance gig work to combat boredom, suddenly introducing volatile self-employment income into your pristine MAGI calculations. You might move to a new state, get married, or realize mid-year that your dividend income is going to be thousands of dollars higher than you projected.

When your income changes in the middle of a Tuesday in October, your healthcare subsidies change with it. If you aren't paying attention, this discrepancy doesn't just disappear—it waits patiently for you at tax time. We will walk through the painful reality of tax reconciliation, where the IRS looks at what you estimated your income would be versus what it actually was, and either hands you a refund or demands you pay back thousands of dollars in excess subsidies. You will build a bulletproof, year-round operating system for tracking your income, updating the Marketplace, and ensuring you never face a massive, unexploded tax bomb in April.

The beauty of the gap years is that they have a hard, predictable finish line. The day you turn 65, this entire complex apparatus vanishes. You transition into the Medicare system, where premiums are no longer tied to MAGI in the same volatile way, and the rules of the game fundamentally shift. Your only job right now is to build a bridge from your last day of work to your sixty-fifth birthday. You just need the bridge to be structurally sound, and you need to cross it without burning through the capital meant to sustain you for the thirty years that follow.

Think of the pages ahead as your engineering manual for that bridge. You do not need to be a certified public accountant or an actuary to master this material. You only need to be willing to look past the intimidating jargon and recognize the straightforward math underneath. Once you grasp how the puzzle pieces fit together—how your dividends affect your premiums, how your cash reserves protect your subsidies, and how a few hours of planning in December can save you ten thousand dollars in January—the anxiety surrounding early retirement healthcare will evaporate.

It will be replaced by something much better: absolute, undeniable control.

The gap years are supposed to be the reward for a lifetime of discipline, saving, and delayed gratification. They are your years to travel, to pivot to passion projects, or simply to wake up on a Tuesday and do absolutely nothing. You have already done the hard work of buying your time back. Now, it is time to protect it. Let's get started.

Chapter 1

Framing the Gap Years and the Healthcare Problem

Retiring before 65 can feel like stepping off the employer-benefits conveyor belt without a map. This chapter gives readers that map. It shows why the gap years deserve their own strategy, how health insurance actually drains or protects a household budget, and why smart planning now can make the road to Medicare far less expensive and far less stressful.

1.1 The Gap Years as a Financial Planning Window

Early retirement is often described as freedom. In one sense, that's true: your calendar opens up. In another sense, it's the first time in decades you're running a small business called "Your Household, Inc." with no benefits department. The biggest surprise for many people isn't boredom or identity. It's the way health coverage stops being a background payroll deduction and starts acting like a major line item that can swing by thousands of dollars based on choices that don't feel like "health choices" at all.

That swinginess is exactly why the gap years deserve to be treated like a distinct planning window. They're not just "retirement, but earlier." They're the years when you're too young for Medicare but no longer sheltered by an employer plan, and when your income is often *more controllable* than it was while you were working. That combination—high stakes, plus new levers—creates an unusual opportunity: you can design a coverage-and-income strategy that works as a system, rather than playing defense every open enrollment season.

The most useful mental shift is to stop thinking of health insurance as a product you buy once a year and start thinking of it as part of a *timeline problem*. You have a known endpoint (Medicare), you have rules that reset annually (Marketplace enrollment and subsidies), and you have household life that doesn't respect calendar boundaries (a spouse keeps working, a kid moves back home, a parent becomes dependent, you relocate, your health changes). Planning is the art of lining those clocks up so they don't collide.

The date you retire is not just a date

"Retiring in June" sounds like a lifestyle decision. In the gap years, it can be a healthcare pricing decision.

The reason is simple: the U.S. health insurance calendar is lumpy. Employer coverage often ends on the last day of the month, or the last day you work, depending on the plan. Marketplace coverage usually runs in monthly chunks. Deductibles and out-of-pocket tracking usually reset with the plan year (often the calendar year). Premium tax credits are reconciled on your tax return based on the year as a whole. So a mid-year retirement can turn one "year" of life into three different insurance realities.

Retire in late December and you might keep employer coverage through year-end, start a Marketplace plan January 1, and get a clean, simple tax year. Retire in March and you might have employer coverage for part of the year, then a Marketplace plan, then the tax reconciliation puzzle where you remember you had two different coverage regimes and one set of household income numbers. Retire in July and you might face the most emotionally irritating scenario of all: paying premiums for the rest of the year while knowing that next January every deductible counter is going back to zero again. It's not "bad," but it changes what kind of plan design feels tolerable.

The retirement date also affects your income story for that year. A final year with wages, a bonus, unused vacation payout, severance, or stock compensation can inflate income and distort Marketplace financial help. That doesn't mean "don't retire then." It means the first gap-year plan may need to be chosen with that one-time income bulge in mind, rather than with the assumption that all gap years look like a steady-state retirement budget.

Household size is a pricing engine, not a demographic detail

Household size sounds like a census question. For ACA purposes, it can function like a pricing engine because it changes how income is measured against the Federal Poverty Level (FPL), and that comparison drives eligibility for premium tax credits and, for many households, cost-sharing reductions.

In plain language: two households with the same income can get very different results if one household is a single person and the other is a couple, or if one includes a dependent who must file a return. The Marketplace doesn't just ask "What do you make?" It effectively asks "What do you make *for a household of your size*?" If you've ever noticed that some families seem to get more help even with similar income, this is often why.

Household composition also changes more often than people expect in early retirement. A child who is still your tax dependent one year and not the next can shift the subsidy math. A spouse who continues working might keep employer coverage, while you move to the Marketplace alone, creating a household with mixed coverage types but one tax return. A divorce or marriage can change everything in one stroke: household size, income, eligibility, and the practical question of whether you can afford to choose a plan with a narrow network.

Early retirement sometimes coincides with caregiving, too. If an aging parent becomes part of your household and tax picture, your healthcare planning can change even if *your* health is stable. The lesson isn't that you must predict every family change. It's that you want a planning process sturdy enough to absorb changes without panic.

State of residence quietly rewrites the menu

Many retirees imagine moving the way they imagine choosing paint colors: a preference, a vibe, a climate. In the gap years, the state line is also a policy line. Marketplace plans are state-based in meaningful ways—different insurers participate, different networks dominate, plan designs vary, and access to providers can shift dramatically. The same "metal tier" label in two different states can feel like two different products.

This matters even if you don't intend to move. Providers move. Insurers exit markets. Networks tighten. One year your favorite hospital is in-network for three options; the next year it's in-network for one, or none. If your plan is built around a particular specialist or a particular health system, you're not just buying insurance—you're buying *access*. And access is local.

If relocation is likely, it's worth treating it as a primary constraint early, not an afterthought. A plan that is "perfect" in your current state may become irrelevant the moment you move. That includes practical details people only learn the hard way: prescriptions can be treated differently, prior authorizations may restart, and a new plan might require you to rebuild your care team. Even your tolerance for administrative friction becomes part of the decision. Some people enjoy optimizing; others just want a plan that doesn't fight them.

The deeper point: early retirement healthcare planning is not only about money. It's about the *shape* of your life. If travel, RV living, or living part-year in another location is your dream, you need to consider how Marketplace networks behave when you're away from home. "Emergency coverage" is not the same as "I can get routine care where I am." That difference is invisible on the premium line and painfully visible when you're trying to book a visit.

Expected healthcare use isn't a guess—it's a scenario set

Most people approach plan selection as if they must forecast the future: "Will I be healthy next year?" That's the wrong question. You don't need a prediction; you need scenarios.

A practical way to think about it is to build three simple pictures of your next year:

- a low-use year (preventive care, a couple of visits, maybe a generic prescription),
- a medium-use year (imaging, physical therapy, specialist visits, ongoing prescriptions),
- a high-use year (an accident, a new diagnosis, surgery, or an expensive medication).

Those scenarios aren't morbid. They're honest. Insurance is a tool for bad luck, and the gap years are often the time when "bad luck" starts getting more statistically plausible—not because you're fragile, but because you're human and you've been alive long enough to have parts that occasionally misbehave.

This scenario approach improves decisions for a surprising reason: it forces you to value the out-of-pocket maximum as a real number, not fine print. There is a hard ceiling on annual in-network cost sharing for essential health benefits in ACA-compliant plans, and CMS publishes that limit each year. For 2026, the maximum annual limitation on cost sharing is $10,150 for self-only coverage and $20,300 for coverage other than self-only. Those numbers are not what most people *expect* to spend; they're what you might be forced to be able to *survive*.

Once you treat that ceiling as part of your financial plan, your plan choice stops being purely emotional. A low-premium plan with a high out-of-pocket ceiling might be completely reasonable if you have cash reserves, low ongoing needs, and a high tolerance for volatility. The same plan can be a slow-motion disaster if a chronic condition makes high use likely, or if your retirement budget is tight enough that a five-figure medical year would cause you to raid accounts in a tax-inefficient way.

And healthcare use isn't only about your body. It's about your habits. If you avoid doctors until something is urgent, a high-deductible design can feel "fine" until it's suddenly very not fine. If you're proactive and like to address issues early, a plan with predictable copays and lower deductibles can be worth a higher premium because it matches how you actually live.

Your cash-flow sources are part of your health insurance strategy

Here's the part that makes the gap years a financial planning window rather than merely a shopping problem: many early retirees have *multiple income spigots*. Wages may stop, but cash flow can come from taxable brokerage accounts, tax-deferred retirement accounts, Roth accounts, Social Security (for some), pensions, rental income, business income, and plain old cash.

Those sources do not behave the same way under ACA rules because Marketplace financial help is tied to a specific definition of income (MAGI for ACA purposes, as you saw earlier). That means the *same* lifestyle—same spending, same vacations, same grocery bill—can produce very different Marketplace outcomes depending on how you fund it.

This is why the gap years can feel upside down the first time you encounter them. In working life, higher income generally meant more options and less worry. In the gap years, higher taxable income can mean less financial help and a much higher net premium. That doesn't make earning or realizing income "bad." It makes it something you schedule and shape.

The most common mistake is to treat account withdrawals like they're morally neutral. "Money is money," so you pull it from wherever feels convenient. But convenience can be expensive. A large withdrawal from a tax-deferred account might cover living expenses beautifully and then quietly raise your Marketplace income enough to shrink premium tax credits—or change other affordability features tied to income. On the other hand, drawing from cash savings or selling assets with favorable tax characteristics might support the same spending with a different income footprint.

It can feel strange to plan income with such care when you're no longer earning a paycheck. The psychological trap is thinking that retirement means you're finally done with "income." You're not. You're just doing income yourself.

One spouse working, one spouse retiring: the household becomes a two-speed machine

A very common gap-years story is the staggered retirement: one spouse is done, the other continues working for a few more years for either income or employer coverage. This scenario looks simple until you try to fit it into a Marketplace application and a tax return.

If the working spouse has access to an employer plan, that plan may be the best option for them. But the retired spouse needs coverage now. Depending on the employer plan and its cost structure, the retired spouse might be able to stay on it, or might face an expensive dependent premium, or might have no access at all. Meanwhile, your household income may still be substantial because one person is earning, which can change the affordability of Marketplace coverage for the other spouse.

Even when the final answer is straightforward—"stay on the employer plan" or "move one spouse to the Marketplace"—the planning work is in the edges:

- Is it worth paying more for administrative simplicity (everyone on one plan) versus splitting coverage?
- If you split coverage, are you comfortable managing two sets of deductibles, networks, and prior authorizations?

- If you're counting on Marketplace subsidies, are you confident you understand how household income interacts with who is enrolled where?

The emotional reality matters too. Two-speed households often have two different risk tolerances. The working spouse may want maximum predictability; the retired spouse may want minimum premiums. Both can be reasonable. The best strategy is usually the one that prevents resentment when the first big medical bill shows up.

Chronic conditions: the "cheap plan" test you can run on day one

If you or a family member has ongoing care needs, Marketplace shopping becomes less about premiums and more about friction: networks, formularies, and the rules that decide whether your care is treated as routine or treated as a negotiation.

A simple way to stress-test a plan is to pick three specific items you know you will use and see how the plan treats them:

1. your primary doctor or specialist (in-network or not),
2. your preferred hospital system (in-network or not),
3. your most important medication (covered, and at what cost tier).

This isn't being picky. It's treating insurance like a contract you'll actually have to live inside.

The gap years make this more important because you're often leaving a familiar employer network and stepping into a world where narrower networks are common. Some plans are excellent values *if* you stay in their ecosystem. Others look affordable until you realize they exclude the providers you trust, which effectively forces you to choose between money and continuity of care. That's not a theoretical trade-off. It's a Tuesday afternoon phone call when the specialist's office says, "We don't take that plan."

If your health is stable today, don't skip this test. People don't choose chronic conditions. They discover them. A plan that is usable only in a narrow slice of your city may be fine until you need the one clinic that isn't included.

Policy volatility is a risk you can't diversify away—so you manage it

Investors are taught to diversify away single-stock risk. ACA Marketplace planning has a kind of risk you can't diversify away: the rules can change.

Subsidy formulas, eligibility thresholds, insurer participation, and plan designs all evolve. Some changes are modest and annoying; others can meaningfully alter what "affordable" means, especially for older enrollees whose premiums are higher due to age rating. The unsettling part is that the change can feel personal—your premium jumps, your plan disappears, your doctors leave the network—but it's rarely personal. It's the system updating.

The practical response isn't to become cynical. It's to build resilience into your plan. Resilience looks like:

- keeping a cash buffer large enough to handle a deductible or a premium increase without blowing up your income strategy,
- avoiding brittle assumptions (for example, that a specific insurer will always be available),
- treating your first Marketplace year as a learning year, with room to adjust.

The goal is not to predict policy. The goal is to avoid being cornered by it.

Make the gap years concrete: build a personal coverage timeline

A timeline turns a vague anxiety ("healthcare is going to be expensive") into a finite project with milestones. Start with two anchors:

the month your employer coverage ends and the month Medicare begins. Then mark the big checkpoints that tend to matter in real life:

- the first open enrollment you'll face without an employer plan,
- any known income spikes (severance, a large Roth conversion you're considering, sale of a property, a year with unusually large capital gains),
- any household shifts you can reasonably anticipate (a dependent aging off, a spouse retiring, a planned move),
- any medical events you're already managing (ongoing prescriptions, scheduled procedures, expected specialist care).

This is not busywork. It's how you keep the gap years from turning into a string of reactive decisions. When you can see the whole bridge from one shore to the other, you stop over-optimizing one year in a way that creates a problem the next year. You also stop treating insurance shopping as a once—a-year endurance test and start treating it as what it really is: an annual update to a longer plan.

The quiet win of the gap years is that you often have more flexibility than you did while working. You can choose when to realize income, when to move, when to schedule elective care, and how to structure your withdrawals. That flexibility can either be wasted—accidentally triggering higher costs—or harnessed to keep coverage affordable and predictable.

Early retirement doesn't come with a benefits department, but it does come with something powerful: time to plan. In the gap years, that time can buy you more than peace of mind. It can buy you real money.

1.2 How Health Insurance Really Costs You Money

Health insurance is one of the only products you buy where the price tag is designed to be incomplete. The monthly premium is real, sure—but it's also a decoy. It's the cover charge to enter a club where the drinks have no menu, the bouncer may or may not recognize your doctor, and the most expensive item is occasionally labeled "patient responsibility" with the casual confidence of a restaurant adding "market price" to lobster.

The gap-year version of this problem is sharper because you're not insulated by payroll deductions and an HR department that quietly picked a plan on your behalf. You're making adult decisions with real adult consequences: how much you pay no matter what, how much you might pay if life gets spicy, and whether the plan you chose actually *works* when you try to use it.

A useful way to think about insurance is that you're buying two things at once:

- a monthly bill you can predict (the premium), and
- a set of rules for what happens when you need care (the cost-sharing and access rules).

If you only compare the monthly bill, you're not shopping—you're hoping.

Premiums: the bill that shows up even when nothing happens

The premium is what you pay to keep the policy active. It's the one cost that doesn't care whether you got sick, exercised, ate kale, or avoided scooters.

Premiums matter because they're guaranteed. A plan with a higher premium is like choosing a higher fixed mortgage payment: it might lower other risks, but it commits you to cash out the door every month. In early retirement, that cash has a personality. Pulling it from a taxable account might trigger capital gains; pulling it from a traditional IRA might create ordinary income; pulling it from cash might feel painless until cash runs low. So a "$300 premium difference" isn't just $300—it's $300 *funded somehow*.

Marketplace premiums also have a habit of being emotionally misread. A plan can look expensive on the screen but be dramatically cheaper *after* premium tax credits. Or it can look cheap and then get expensive when credits shrink because income comes in higher than expected. Either way, the premium you pay is often the result of a tax-credit math problem, not just the insurer's sticker price.

Deductibles: the spending threshold where insurance stops being decorative

A deductible is the amount you generally pay for covered services before the plan starts paying in a meaningful way. Think of it as the "you're on your own" layer.

Deductibles create the classic early-retiree whiplash: you can have insurance and still feel uninsured for routine care. That's not a flaw in your perception; it's literally how many plan designs work. A high-deductible plan can be a great financial deal in a quiet year, but it turns the first several thousand dollars of care into a personal cash-flow event.

The practical takeaway is not "avoid deductibles." Deductibles are a lever. They trade monthly premium for pay-as-you-go exposure. The question is whether you want that exposure, whether you can fund it without tax chaos, and whether it matches your likely year of care.

One subtle point: deductibles are usually annual. They reset. Your body does not. If you schedule care across year-end—say, imaging in December and follow-up in January—you can pay the "first-dollar" deductible layer twice. That doesn't mean you should rush medical decisions into the calendar. It means the plan year can create accidental cost spikes.

Copays: the flat fees that feel simple (until they aren't)

A copay is a fixed amount you pay for a service—$30 for a primary care visit, $75 for a specialist, $15 for a generic prescription, and so on. Copays are popular because they're predictable. If you like budgeting, copays feel like sanity.

Copays come with two gotchas. First, copays often apply *after* you meet a deductible on some plans, meaning the plan's marketing language ("$40 specialist copay!") can be functionally irrelevant until you've already paid thousands out of pocket. Second, copays are only as good as the network and the formulary. A $40 copay for a specialist who won't accept your plan is like a coupon for a store in another state.

Coinsurance: the percentage that turns into big numbers fast

Coinsurance is the percentage of allowed charges you pay after meeting your deductible. A plan might say "20% coinsurance," which sounds manageable until you do the math on real medical prices. Twenty percent of a $2,000 outpatient procedure is $400. Twenty percent of a $30,000 surgery is not a cute number.

Coinsurance is why "I'm healthy" can be an unreliable plan design strategy. You might be healthy and still get blindsided by a single event—a fall, an appendix, a weird scan that turns into more scans. Coinsurance is also why it's dangerous to evaluate plans using only the deductible. Two plans can have similar deductibles and wildly different coinsurance, which changes what happens in the messy middle of a medium-to-high usage year.

If deductibles define when insurance starts helping, coinsurance defines how generously it helps once it does.

Out-of-pocket maximums: the damage-control ceiling

The out-of-pocket maximum (often shortened to MOOP) is the most you are required to pay in a plan year for covered in-network services for essential health benefits, excluding premiums. Once you hit that number, the plan pays 100% of covered in-network costs for the rest of the year.

This is the part of the contract that turns medical catastrophe into a financial problem you can at least *bound*. It's not a pleasant number, but it is a number you can plan around—especially important in the gap years, when you may not have wages to refill your checking account after an ugly medical year.

CMS publishes the ACA annual maximum annual limitation on cost sharing. For 2026, it's $10,150 for self-only coverage and $20,300 for coverage other than self-only. Those are ceilings, not targets. But they're also not theoretical. If you choose a plan with a high MOOP, you're implicitly saying: "If I have a really bad year, I can write checks up to this amount (plus premiums) without detonating the rest of my plan."

Two clarifiers save a lot of heartbreak:

- The MOOP generally applies to *covered, in-network* care. Out-of-network bills can behave very differently.
- Premiums are separate. The MOOP is a ceiling on cost-sharing, not on total annual spending for health insurance.

Networks: the quiet way a "cheap" plan becomes expensive

A provider network is the list of doctors, hospitals, labs, and facilities that have contracts with your insurer. Inside the network, prices are negotiated and your plan rules apply. Outside the network, your costs can spike, sometimes dramatically, and the rules can become a thicket of exceptions and partial reimbursements.

Networks matter even if you don't think you "care about doctors." When you need care, you tend to care about three things very quickly:

- Can I get an appointment without waiting forever?
- Can I go to the hospital system I trust (or the one closest to me)?
- Will this be treated as in-network so the MOOP actually protects me?

Early retirees often discover that network breadth is something you're paying for, like legroom on an airplane. Narrower networks can be a rational design choice for insurers and can produce lower premiums. They can also produce the maddening experience of having "insurance" that doesn't include the providers you'd naturally use.

The shopping move here is simple but non-negotiable: before you fall in love with a premium, check whether the plan includes your must-have providers and facilities. If you don't have must-haves, pick one or two "likely" providers and check anyway. A plan that breaks the moment you try to use it is not a bargain.

Drug formularies: where the same medication can cost $10 or $300

A drug formulary is the insurer's list of covered medications, organized into tiers. Lower tiers tend to be cheaper; higher tiers tend to have higher copays or coinsurance. Some drugs require prior authorization. Some have quantity limits. Some are covered only if you try a different medication first (step therapy). These rules can feel like bureaucracy until you're the one standing at the pharmacy counter.

Formularies matter because prescriptions are the most predictable kind of healthcare use. People rarely wake up and spontaneously need a new daily medication for fun. If you take a maintenance drug, you already know what you'll be buying twelve times a year. A plan that treats that drug harshly is like a landlord charging extra for electricity in a place where you work from home.

Even if you don't take regular medications today, it's worth understanding how your plan handles drugs because a new diagnosis can turn pharmacy costs into the main event. Many people think "the big risk is the hospital." Sometimes it's the medication that follows you home.

Cost-sharing reductions: the hidden upgrade that only exists at certain incomes

Cost-sharing reductions (CSRs) are one of the most misunderstood features of the Marketplace because they don't sound like money. They sound like paperwork.

CSRs reduce deductibles, copays, and coinsurance—meaning they reduce what you pay *when you use care*. The catch is that CSRs are only available if you enroll in a Silver plan and meet the income rules for CSR eligibility. Two people can both say "I have a Silver plan" and have radically different real-world protection because one is on a CSR-eligible Silver variant and the other is on standard Silver.

This is why "cheap premium" can be a trap in the gap years. Sometimes the best deal is not the plan with the lowest premium; it's the plan that gives you the best protection against out-of-pocket costs for the income level you're targeting. If you're doing any kind of income management, CSRs are one of the reasons the effort can pay off in more than one way.

Putting the pieces together: predictable cost vs. worst-case cost

There's a reason health insurance feels hard to compare: each plan is a different mix of fixed costs and conditional costs. One plan is like paying more rent for an apartment with utilities included. Another is like paying low rent and then discovering the building charges separately for heat, water, trash, and the privilege of opening a window.

A clean way to compare plans is to look through two lenses at the same time:

- *Predictable annual cost*: the premium you'll pay no matter what, plus what you're likely to pay in a low-use year.
- *Worst-case annual cost*: the premium plus the out-of-pocket maximum (because that's the ceiling in a bad year for covered in-network care).

Medium-use years are the tie-breakers. Many households don't have "perfectly healthy" years forever, and most don't hit the MOOP every year either. The plans that look close on paper can behave very differently in the middle: an MRI here, a specialist there, a physical therapy run, a new prescription, an outpatient procedure, and suddenly you're living in the fine print.

The point isn't to scare you into buying the richest plan available. The point is to make sure you're consciously buying a mix of premium and risk that you can carry without resentment—or without forcing yourself into tax moves you didn't want to make.

The buyer's checklist hiding inside the jargon

Once the vocabulary clicks, plan evaluation gets less mystical. You stop asking "Is this plan good?" and start asking questions a buyer would ask:

- What do I pay even if nothing happens? (Premium.)
- What do I pay in the first meaningful stretch of care? (Deductible.)
- After that, how does the bill split? (Copays and coinsurance.)
- Where does the bleeding stop in a bad year? (Out-of-pocket maximum, plus premiums.)

- Will I be allowed to use the doctors and hospitals I'd naturally use? (Network.)
- Will my medications be treated like routine purchases or luxury goods? (Formulary.)

People sometimes feel embarrassed asking these questions, as if everyone else is effortlessly fluent and they missed the day in school when health insurance was explained. In reality, most people are guessing. The industry benefits from guessers. The gap years reward buyers.

The last move is psychological: resist the urge to crown a plan "the winner" based on a single number. Health insurance is a bundle of trade-offs, and the right bundle depends on how you fund your life, how much financial volatility you can tolerate, and how much administrative friction you're willing to endure. When you can name the pieces, you can choose the trade-off on purpose—and that's where the money starts staying in your accounts instead of evaporating into surprises.

1.3 Planning Backward from Medicare

Most people treat Medicare like a far-off appliance manual: they know it exists, they assume it will work when the time comes, and they'd rather not read the instructions until smoke appears. That attitude is understandable. It's also expensive in exactly the way early retirees hate—expensive through timing mistakes, paperwork friction, and penalties that don't feel connected to any real benefit you received.

Age 65 is not just a birthday in the gap years. It's a hard cutoff where one system stops and another begins. The problem is that the hand-off isn't automatic for everyone, and it isn't always graceful even when you do everything right. The household that thinks about the Medicare transition early gets to make calm, strategic choices. The household that thinks about it late is more likely to buy overlapping coverage, accidentally create a gap, or discover that a "small delay" has a lifetime price tag.

Medicare is a deadline with a calendar, not a vibe

Medicare has a built-in runway called the *Initial Enrollment Period.* The Medicare Initial Enrollment Period lasts 7 months (3 months before turning 65 through 3 months after). That sentence carries more practical power than most retirement calculators.

Seven months sounds generous until you remember what you're doing during those months: comparing options, deciding when to start, coordinating with existing coverage, and making sure the paperwork lands cleanly so coverage begins when you think it begins. Every one of those steps can be slowed down by ordinary life—travel, family events, a move, an illness, even just procrastination.

The deeper point is that Medicare is not like flipping a switch from "ACA plan" to "Medicare plan" on your birthday. It's more like changing planes at an airport you've never visited. The connection can be smooth, but only if you understand which gate you need and when boarding starts.

The last pre-65 year is where small errors get loud

Early retirees often put the most energy into the first year after leaving work: figuring out the Marketplace, estimating income, choosing between lower premium and lower out-of-pocket risk. That's sensible. But the final Marketplace year before Medicare often requires more attention, not less.

Why? Because you're coordinating an exit. You're not simply choosing a plan; you're choosing a plan that needs to end neatly. Coverage start dates and end dates matter more. Your deductible reset matters more. Your income strategy matters more because the year contains both "pre-Medicare life" and "Medicare life," and those halves can interact in awkward ways.

This is the year when "I'll deal with it later" tends to produce some combination of annoyance and money leaving your pocket. Not dramatic, cinematic money. Just the slow bleed of duplicate premiums, uncovered weeks, or administrative confusion that turns your mailbox into a part-time job.

Avoiding coverage gaps around the birthday month

A coverage gap is the dullest kind of crisis. Nobody is calling an ambulance because your policy started on the wrong date. You find out when you go to pick up a prescription, schedule a procedure, or receive a bill that says "Denied: no coverage." It's one of the few financial mistakes that can happen silently and then arrive as a surprise invoice.

The fix is conceptually simple: decide in advance when Medicare should start, and then make sure your other coverage ends in a way that doesn't leave an uncovered day. The execution can be tricky because different systems have different clocks. Employer plans might end when employment ends or at month-end. Marketplace coverage typically runs on monthly cycles. Medicare start timing depends on when you enroll and which part you're starting.

This is also where people accidentally pay twice. Paying for overlapping coverage is sometimes unavoidable for a short period, and occasionally it's worth it for peace of mind. But it should be a deliberate purchase, not a byproduct of uncertainty. If you do end up with overlap, treat it as a short bridge with a clear end date—not as a lingering subscription you forget to cancel.

Part B is the "don't mess around" part for early retirees

Medicare is not one monolithic plan; it's a set of parts with different roles. The part that tends to cause the most trouble in early-retirement transitions is Part B (medical insurance), because timing mistakes can stick.

Part B late enrollment penalties can apply when enrollment is delayed without qualifying coverage; Medicare.gov describes the penalty concept as increasing by 10% for each full 12-month period of delay. That's not a one-time fee you swallow and move on from. It's the kind of penalty that follows you, year after year, attached to a premium you'll pay for a long time.

This is where "qualifying coverage" becomes a make-or-break phrase. Some people delay Part B because they still have coverage through work (their own or a spouse's) and are allowed to do so without penalty. Others delay because they assume their existing non-Medicare coverage counts as the right kind of coverage, or because they're trying to avoid paying an extra premium, or because the forms feel confusing. The penalty risk is not meant to be punitive; it's meant to enforce the idea that Medicare is a coordinated system that expects you to enter at a certain time unless you have the right reason not to.

The planning move is to treat Part B timing as a decision with consequences, not as a checkbox. If you are delaying, you want to be very confident you have the kind of coverage that makes delaying safe. If you are not delaying, you want to be very confident you are enrolling early enough that Part B starts when you need it.

Medigap timing: the window that doesn't care if you're busy

Many people think of Medicare planning as "pick a plan." But one of the most time-sensitive parts is not the plan itself; it's a purchase window.

Medigap planning is time-sensitive: the Medigap Open Enrollment Period is 6 months starting the first month you have Part B and are age 65+; during this period you have stronger purchase protections.

Translation: you get a special season where shopping is easier and your health history generally has less power over your options.

This is a rare moment in insurance where timing can improve fairness. Outside that window, the rules can be stricter depending on your circumstances and location. Inside it, you're more likely to be treated like a standard buyer.

The gap-years implication is straightforward: Part B timing isn't only about Part B. It can also be about protecting your ability to choose Medigap coverage under the best possible conditions. Put differently, a delayed or messy Part B start doesn't merely delay coverage; it can shift when (or whether) you get that Medigap purchase window, and that can echo for years.

When one spouse hits Medicare first, your household splits into two systems

A common real-life scenario is the age gap: one spouse turns 65 while the other is still years away. At that moment, your household can end up running two separate healthcare machines at once—Medicare for one person, Marketplace coverage (or other coverage) for the other.

This is where planning backward pays dividends because it prevents "surprise complexity." You may need to think about:

- whether the younger spouse's coverage stays the same or needs a reset,
- how household income planning interacts with Marketplace help for the younger spouse,
- how provider access works when one spouse has Medicare networks and the other has an ACA plan network.

The emotional friction point is that couples are used to sharing a plan the way they share a phone bill. Suddenly they may not be able to. The administrative friction point is that you now have two ID cards, two sets of explanations of benefits, two deductibles (if applicable), and possibly two different philosophies of what is "in-network."

The financial friction point is subtler: the household may be tempted to treat the Medicare transition as a moment when "healthcare gets cheaper now." Sometimes it does. Sometimes it doesn't, especially when you still have one person buying pre-65 coverage with age-rated premiums. The right expectation is not "cheaper"; it's "different."

The final Marketplace year: treat income and medical timing like they're connected (because they are)

During the gap years, income strategy and healthcare strategy are entangled, whether you want them to be or not. In the final year before Medicare, that entanglement tightens.

One reason is psychological: people often want to do "one last big financial move" before 65—sell investments, do a larger Roth conversion, harvest gains, or reposition assets. Those moves can be smart. They can also create a one-year spike in income that collides with Marketplace subsidies and changes your net premium during that same year. If you're doing Marketplace coverage up until Medicare starts, the timing of income matters.

Another reason is practical medical timing. People sometimes try to schedule elective care before Medicare begins because they want it handled under the system they already understand, or because they've already met a deductible on the ACA plan, or because their providers are in-network now and they fear disruptions later. Those instincts can be rational. But they're also the kind of instincts that work best when paired with a calendar that includes enrollment windows and start dates, not just appointment dates.

The goal isn't to micromanage your health around insurance. The goal is to avoid being forced into bad timing. If you have flexibility, use it. If you don't, at least know what deadlines you're up against so you don't accidentally create a gap when you're least interested in paperwork.

A practical Medicare transition checklist for the final 12 months

A checklist turns Medicare from a looming event into a series of small, boring tasks—which is exactly what you want. The point is not to become a Medicare scholar. The point is to prevent the two classic failure modes: delayed enrollment with penalty risk, and coverage gaps caused by mismatched start and end dates.

Here is a simple way to stage your thinking:

About 12 months before turning 65

Start acting like the year has edges.

- Confirm when your current coverage can end and what triggers that end (month-end, termination date, voluntary cancellation).
- Sketch the income moves you *might* want to make in the final pre-65 year so you can see whether you're setting up an accidental subsidy swing.
- If you're planning a move, treat it as a healthcare event, not just a real estate event—because provider access and plan availability are local.

About 6 months before turning 65

Turn vague preferences into decisions you can execute.

- Decide whether you expect Medicare to start at 65 or whether you have a legitimate reason to delay Part B.

- If one spouse will remain on pre-65 coverage, map out how the household will handle two systems without missing premium payments or enrollment steps.
- Take inventory of any ongoing care (specialists, prescriptions, scheduled procedures) that could be disrupted by a network change, so you can plan for continuity.

About 3 months before turning 65

Treat this like boarding time, not shopping time.

- Use the Initial Enrollment Period window intentionally; remember it begins 3 months before turning 65.
- If you are enrolling in Part B, do it early enough that the start date aligns with your desired end date for other coverage.
- If you intend to buy Medigap, remember the Medigap Open Enrollment Period is tied to when you have Part B and are age 65+, and it lasts 6 months.

This checklist is intentionally plain. Medicare becomes stressful when people let it remain conceptual until the last minute. When you turn it into deadlines, the stress usually drops.

The real benefit of backward planning: keeping options open

Planning backward from Medicare is less about perfection and more about preserving optionality. If you enroll on time, you keep yourself out of penalty territory. If you coordinate start and end dates, you reduce the chance of uncovered days or wasted premiums. If you treat the Medigap window as a serious calendar event, you give yourself the best shot at buying the coverage you want under the strongest purchase protections.

The gap years are full of levers—income levers, withdrawal levers, plan-choice levers. Medicare is the point where many of those levers change shape. The households that do well are not the ones who memorize every rule. They're the ones who respect the calendar, treat timing as a financial variable, and refuse to let a birthday become an administrative surprise.

1.4 A Decision Framework for Affordable Coverage

Open enrollment has a talent for turning rational adults into frantic clickers. One tab with plan brochures, another with a provider directory that times out, a third with last year's premium, and a fourth where you're trying to remember whether your spouse's birthday changes anything. The system is noisy on purpose. A framework is how you turn the volume down.

The goal isn't to find a mythical "best plan." The goal is to make a series of choices in the right order so you don't accidentally optimize the wrong thing. Most expensive mistakes in pre-65 coverage aren't caused by picking a "bad" plan; they're caused by picking a plan before you've decided what income you're going to show on paper, or by choosing a premium based on hope instead of worst-case exposure, or by discovering too late that the plan doesn't include the hospital system you'd use if something went wrong.

Affordable coverage decisions in the gap years are a three-part optimization: (1) eligibility and size of premium tax credit (MAGI-driven), (2) eligibility for CSR (income-driven and Silver-only), and (3) plan design risk (deductible/coinsurance/network) bounded by MOOP. That sentence is dense, but it's also liberating: it tells you what matters, what drives what, and where the hard limits are.

Here's the repeatable sequence that keeps you out of the most common traps.

Step 1: Start with the coverage paths you actually have

Before you compare deductibles, you want to know what universe you're shopping in. People often jump straight to Marketplace plans because that's the loudest option. But the first question is more basic: what coverage paths are available *to your household* this year?

In practice, most households are choosing among a short list: employer coverage for a working spouse, a retiree plan if you have one, COBRA for a temporary bridge, Marketplace coverage, or (less commonly) some other qualifying coverage arrangement. The reason to identify the path first is that it determines what kinds of trade-offs even exist. A Marketplace plan is a lever-rich system: income affects premium tax credits and potentially CSRs, plan choice affects networks and out-of-pocket exposure, and all of it gets reconciled at tax time. Employer coverage is usually simpler but can be expensive for a spouse or dependent. COBRA can be a relief valve—same plan, same network—but often at a higher premium.

The point is not to list every option under the sun. It's to avoid spending hours comparing Marketplace plans when the correct answer is "stay on the spouse's employer plan," or assuming COBRA is unaffordable when it may be the cleanest bridge for a few months, or forgetting that you may be making different decisions for different household members.

If the household is split—one person on Medicare, one person not; one person working, one person not—treat that as normal, not as a complication you'll "solve later." It's a legitimate design constraint, like having two cars with different fuel types. You don't argue with reality; you plan around it.

Step 2: Pick a target income range before you shop plans

Marketplace affordability is not just about what you spend. It's about what the system thinks you earn. That's why people can have the same lifestyle and wildly different premiums: one household is pulling from a source that increases MAGI, another is living off cash or tax-efficient sources, and the Marketplace math responds.

MAGI definitions and household composition rules are central; small differences in what counts as income or who is in the tax household can change subsidy eligibility. This is where "close enough" can become a surprisingly expensive philosophy.

A good planning habit is to set an income target *range*, not a single number. Real life moves. Dividends show up. Capital gains happen. A part-time consulting job turns out to be more fun than expected. A Roth conversion you planned in November gets pushed into December. If your plan requires hitting an exact income number, it isn't a plan; it's a tightrope.

An income range does two things. First, it gives you room to make normal life decisions without constantly worrying you've broken your health coverage. Second, it turns open enrollment into a more coherent comparison because you're evaluating plans under the subsidy rules you expect to live under, not under last year's income or a guess you made in a hurry.

If you're thinking, "But I don't know what my income will be," that's the point. The best you can do is estimate, track, and adjust. You're not aiming for clairvoyance; you're building a system that can handle updates.

Step 3: Decide how subsidy-sensitive you want your year to be

Some households prefer stability: they'd rather pay a bit more than deal with the possibility of a big premium tax credit reconciliation surprise at tax time. Others are willing to run closer to a threshold because the savings are meaningful and they can manage the income levers.

Subsidy-sensitivity is a real risk dimension, like stock allocation. If your plan depends on staying within a narrow income band, you need the temperament and the tools to monitor that band. If your plan is robust across a wider band, you may spend more but sleep better.

This is also where CSRs can change the entire feel of a plan. Because CSRs reduce deductibles, copays, and coinsurance—but only on a Silver plan—your targeted income range can indirectly steer you toward (or away from) Silver even if you walked in assuming you'd buy Bronze or Gold. The Marketplace is one of the few places where your "income strategy" can change not only the premium you pay but also the size of the bills you face when you get care.

If you've never experienced a CSR-boosted Silver plan, it can be startling: the deductible and out-of-pocket maximum can look like a completely different product. That isn't marketing. It's policy. And it means the plan comparison you do without thinking about income can be the wrong comparison.

Step 4: Choose your risk posture using two numbers: expected cost and worst case

By now you've narrowed the universe. You know your coverage path. You have a target income range. You have a sense of how much you want to depend on subsidies and CSRs. Now you can compare plans in a way that mirrors reality rather than advertising.

Use two numbers for each plan:

- *Expected annual cost*: net premiums (after any premium tax credit effect) plus a reasonable estimate of out-of-pocket costs in a normal year for you.
- *Worst-case annual cost*: net premiums plus the out-of-pocket maximum (MOOP).

The first number answers: "What does a typical year cost?" The second answers: "If the year goes sideways, what is the maximum I can be asked to pay for covered in-network care, besides premiums?" Those two numbers are the heart of medical risk budgeting.

Official parameters (e.g., MOOP limits) provide a hard ceiling on in-network essential-health-benefit cost sharing, which can be used to frame worst-case annual exposure. That ceiling is a gift from a planning perspective. It turns a potentially infinite risk into a finite one. Finite doesn't mean small. It means you can build it into your cash reserves, your withdrawal plan, and your peace of mind.

This step is also where people discover their real preferences. Some households hate variability; they would rather pay higher premiums and have fewer surprises when they use care. Others are comfortable with a higher deductible because they have cash reserves and expect low utilization. Neither is morally superior. But mixing a "high variability" plan with a "low variability" household budget is a recipe for stress.

If you're a numbers person, the comparison is straightforward. If you're not, ask one question: "If I had to pay the worst-case number next year, would that force me to do something financially ugly?" "Ugly" might mean draining the emergency fund, selling investments at a bad time, triggering extra taxable income that increases your Marketplace income, or pulling large amounts from tax-deferred accounts when you were trying to manage brackets. If the answer is yes, you're buying a plan that assumes you'll be lucky.

Step 5: Run the plan through the real-world filters: network and drugs

This is the step people skip because it's annoying. It's also the step that keeps a plan from turning into a disappointment.

A plan with a gorgeous premium and a tolerable MOOP can still fail you if the network is unusable or the formulary treats your medications harshly. And "unusable" doesn't just mean your favorite doctor is out of network. It can mean the nearest in-network hospital is not the one you'd want in a serious situation. It can mean the specialists in-network have long waits. It can mean the plan's preferred pharmacy setup turns refills into a monthly hassle.

Network and formulary checking is like inspecting the foundation of a house. You don't do it because it's fun. You do it because regret is more expensive.

A quick, pragmatic approach:

- Check at least one primary care practice, one local hospital system, and any specialist you'd hate to lose.
- Check your key prescriptions and any "maybe soon" prescriptions (for example, common medications related to conditions in your family).

If you don't have providers you're attached to, pick the providers you'd likely use—nearby, reputable, convenient—and verify the plan doesn't quietly exclude them.

This step also forces honesty about how you access care. If you travel for months at a time, a tight local network might be fine for emergencies but frustrating for routine care. If you live in an area with one dominant health system, a plan that doesn't contract with it can be effectively unusable even if it is technically "insurance."

Step 6: Build an annual operating rhythm: estimate, track, update, tune

A plan chosen in November is not a plan executed by itself. The Marketplace year is alive. Income changes. Household composition changes. Work shows up. Dividends show up. The plan that was perfect at the beginning of the year can become misaligned by August.

A solid operating rhythm has four parts:

Estimate

Start the year with an income estimate that matches the reality of your accounts and your likely withdrawals. If you're living off a mix of taxable and retirement accounts, your estimate should reflect not only spending but *how* you're funding spending.

Track

Do a simple quarterly check-in. Not because you love spreadsheets, but because you'd rather steer than swerve. Tracking helps you notice when you're drifting toward a reconciliation surprise. It also helps you plan intentional moves—harvesting gains, doing a Roth conversion, taking an IRA distribution—rather than doing them impulsively in December.

Update

When income changes materially, update the Marketplace application. That sentence can trigger groans because nobody enjoys updating the application. But it's the mechanism by which premium tax credits are adjusted during the year. Skipping updates is a common way people end up with either a big repayment at tax time or missed credits they could have used.

Tune

Near year-end, you may have the ability to fine-tune income—deciding whether to realize gains now or next year, deciding whether to do a conversion this year or postpone, deciding which accounts to draw from for the last few months. This is where your healthcare plan and tax plan become the same plan. The goal is not to contort your life around MAGI; it's to avoid sleepwalking into a number you didn't intend.

This rhythm turns the Marketplace from an annual cliff into a manageable process. It's the difference between "We'll see what happens" and "We're running this."

Step 7: Plan for change without rebuilding your brain every year

The best framework is reusable. You shouldn't have to re-learn the entire system each open enrollment season. You want a one-page worksheet—literal paper or digital—that you can revisit annually.

At minimum, that worksheet should capture:

- coverage path options available this year,
- expected household size and any anticipated changes,
- target income range (MAGI-based),
- whether CSRs are likely to matter (and therefore whether Silver deserves special attention),
- plan comparison using expected annual cost and worst-case annual cost,
- network and formulary checks for the short list.

What makes the worksheet powerful is not the paper. It's the way it prevents you from making the same mistake twice. It also helps both spouses see the logic. Healthcare decisions can become emotionally loaded—especially when one person wants the cheapest premium and the other wants the strongest protection. A framework gives you a shared language for trade-offs instead of a debate conducted entirely in gut feelings.

The hidden win: integrating healthcare with the rest of the retirement plan

Healthcare planning in the pre-Medicare window is often treated as an annoying side quest. It isn't. It's a central part of cash-flow planning, tax planning, and risk management.

A plan with a low premium but high worst-case exposure might require you to hold more cash than you otherwise would. A plan that is heavily subsidy-dependent may require you to be more deliberate about which accounts you spend from and when. A plan with strong

CSR protection might change the way you think about "how much risk we can afford to self-insure."

Once you see the links, you stop treating health insurance as a bill and start treating it as a design choice. That design choice can either fight your retirement strategy or reinforce it.

The whole point of a decision framework is to make the trade-offs explicit. When you can name the levers—coverage path, income range, subsidy sensitivity, plan risk, and usability—you're no longer at the mercy of whatever plan looks cheapest on a website that day. You're buying coverage like an owner, not like a bystander.

Chapter 2

How the ACA Marketplace Works for Early Retirees

Retiring before 65 can feel like stepping off the employer-insurance conveyor belt and into a system written in another language. The good news is that the ACA Marketplace is learnable. Once you understand the small set of rules that drive eligibility, enrollment, subsidies, and tax cleanup later, you can stop guessing and start making deliberate choices that protect both your health coverage and your retirement cash flow.

2.1 Who Can Use the Marketplace and What Can Block Financial Help

The Marketplace is often described like an emergency room for the uninsured. In practice, it's closer to a well-lit bridge with toll discounts for people who follow the rules. If you leave work at 58 with a paid-off house, a tidy taxable account, and a calendar full of hiking trips, you can still use the Marketplace as your main health plan—*and* you can sometimes make it surprisingly affordable. But there's a catch that trips up organized people: eligibility to *buy* a plan is broad; eligibility for *financial help* is picky. The "picky" part isn't moral judgment. It's just how the law prevents double-dipping when you already have access to other coverage.

A good mental model is this: there are two doors. Door #1 is "Can I enroll in a Marketplace plan?" Door #2 is "Can I get the monthly discount that makes the premium feel sane?" Many households walk through Door #1, assume Door #2 will open automatically, and then discover—often mid-application—that they've been quietly carrying a key that locks it.

Door #1: Who can buy a Marketplace plan?

For most people retiring before 65, Door #1 is straightforward. You generally can enroll if you live in the U.S., are a U.S. citizen or lawfully present, and aren't incarcerated. The Marketplace is designed for ordinary households in ordinary situations: self-employed, in-between jobs, living off investments, or simply done with full-time work.

The part that's less obvious is that "available to you" is not the same as "a good idea for you." You can usually *purchase* a Marketplace plan even when you have other options on the table. The Marketplace doesn't police your decision the way a bouncer checks IDs; it asks questions, runs the eligibility logic, and then tells you whether you qualify for reduced premiums and/or extra help with deductibles and copays. You can still choose to enroll without the discount—many people do—but you should do it with eyes open because unsubsidized premiums can be startlingly high, especially for people in their late 50s and early 60s.

Door #2: The discount comes with strings

The monthly discount (the advance version of the tax credit) is not a "coupon for shoppers." It's a tool meant for households who *don't have access* to other qualifying coverage. That's why the most important pre-shopping question isn't "Which plan has the lowest premium?" It's "Is there anything about our situation that disqualifies us from financial help?"

Those disqualifiers are easy to miss because they often sound like good news: "My spouse can add me at work." "I could stay on COBRA." "I can enroll in Medicare soon." "Our income might be low enough for Medicaid." Any one of those can change the answer from "discount available" to "full price."

The practical trick is to treat subsidy eligibility as an on/off gate you verify *before* you fall in love with a plan design or network.

Minimum essential coverage: a bureaucratic phrase with real-world teeth

"Minimum essential coverage" (MEC) is one of those phrases that makes your brain slide off the page. In everyday life, it means: coverage the government recognizes as real health insurance for purposes of ACA rules. If you have MEC for a month, that month generally isn't a month the Marketplace discount is meant to subsidize.

Two nuances matter:

- MEC isn't the same as "good coverage." A plan can count as MEC and still have frustrating networks, high deductibles, or awkward rules. The government's question is not "Will you love this plan?" It's "Is this the kind of coverage that makes you ineligible for Marketplace financial help?"
- *Eligibility* for certain kinds of coverage can matter as much as *enrollment*. This is where people get blindsided: you can be blocked from the discount even if you never actually sign up for the other coverage.

That second point is the landmine. Imagine turning down a spouse's employer plan because you'd rather pick your own doctors—reasonable!—and then learning the Marketplace will charge you full freight because you *could have* taken the employer plan. The Marketplace isn't punishing a preference; it's applying a rule.

The biggest subsidy blocker: an offer of employer coverage that's "affordable" and provides "minimum value"

For people stepping away from work, the most common subsidy blocker isn't Medicare or Medicaid. It's an employer plan—yours or your spouse's.

The key idea: if someone in your tax household is offered job-based coverage that is considered *affordable* and provides *minimum value,* that person generally can't receive the Marketplace discount—even if they decline the employer plan and even if they enroll in a Marketplace plan anyway.

Those two terms carry specific meanings:

- *Affordable* doesn't mean "comfortable for our budget." It's a test based on the premium you'd pay (under the rule's definition) compared to household income.
- *Minimum value* is a basic adequacy standard—again, not perfection, but a minimum threshold the plan is expected to meet.

Here's why this matters in retirement planning language: people often assume the Marketplace discount is based only on income. Income is necessary, but it's not sufficient. You can engineer your income beautifully and still end up paying full price if an employer offer is sitting on the table and it passes the affordability/minimum-value tests.

Spouse coverage counts. This is the version that surprises couples. One spouse retires at 60. The other keeps working at a job with benefits. The working spouse casually says, "We can put you on my plan." If that plan is deemed affordable and meets minimum value, the retiree may be blocked from Marketplace financial help. That doesn't make the spouse plan automatically better—it might have a narrow network or a higher premium—but it changes the math. You're no longer comparing "subsidized Marketplace vs. spouse plan." You're comparing "full-price Marketplace vs. spouse plan."

A useful way to think about it: the Marketplace discount is designed as a substitute for employer help with premiums. If employer help is available under the rules, the Marketplace steps back.

COBRA: not a subsidy blocker by itself, but it can still trip you

COBRA sits in a weird middle ground. It's not "an employer plan you're actively working under," but it is continuation of job-based coverage.

Two practical rules cover most real decisions:

- Being *offered* COBRA generally does not, by itself, disqualify you from Marketplace financial help. Many people leaving a job can choose Marketplace coverage and, if otherwise eligible, still get the discount.
- Being *enrolled* in COBRA for a month generally means that month is not a month for Marketplace financial help. You typically can't double up.

This is why COBRA can cause accidental whiplash. A common storyline looks like this:

> You retire in June. HR offers COBRA, and you take it "for now" while you shop. In October you decide the Marketplace looks better and switch during open enrollment or a special enrollment window. At tax time, you're confused why the monthly discount didn't apply earlier in the year.

The fix isn't complicated—it's mostly about planning the handoff. If your goal is subsidized Marketplace coverage, treat COBRA as a deliberate bridge for a defined period, not the default setting you flip on and forget.

Medicare: when you're eligible, the discount door closes

Medicare has a clean, unforgiving interaction with Marketplace financial help. If you're eligible for Medicare, the Marketplace is not designed to subsidize you. Even if you *prefer* a Marketplace plan, even if you haven't enrolled in Medicare yet, Medicare eligibility is a bright line in the rules.

That matters for two kinds of households:

- Someone turning 65 mid-year. The planning isn't just "sign up for Medicare." It's "avoid creating months where you expect Marketplace discounts but are Medicare-eligible."
- A spouse who becomes Medicare-eligible while the other spouse is still shopping on the Marketplace. One spouse can be in Medicare while the other remains on the Marketplace; the financial help calculation and household situation can feel counterintuitive if you're not expecting it.

The emotional trap is thinking of Medicare as a "plan choice." In the subsidy logic, it's closer to a status change. Once you're on the Medicare side of the fence, the Marketplace discount isn't meant for you.

Medicaid and CHIP: great coverage, but it changes your Marketplace role

If employer coverage is the most common blocker, Medicaid is the most misunderstood one. People hear "Medicaid" and imagine a completely different world—paperwork, asset limits, stigma, or the fear that it's only for someone in crisis. But for adults with low income, Medicaid can be exactly what the system intends: comprehensive coverage with low out-of-pocket costs.

When you're eligible for Medicaid (or, for children, CHIP), you generally aren't eligible for Marketplace financial help for that person.

In other words, the Marketplace discount is not meant to be the back door to coverage if Medicaid is the front door.

This matters in households with lumpy retirement income. A year with low realized income—maybe you live off cash, dividends, and basis, or you postpone capital gains—can shift you toward Medicaid eligibility depending on your state. Some households are thrilled. Others are frustrated because they expected a Marketplace plan with a certain network. Neither reaction is wrong; the important part is seeing it coming so you can plan rather than improvise.

Also note the family dimension: eligibility can differ within the same household. Children might qualify for CHIP while adults use the Marketplace, or one adult might qualify for Medicaid while another does not. The system can split the household across programs.

Other government coverage that can block financial help

Several other kinds of coverage can function like a "financial help blocker" because they're considered qualifying coverage. In practical terms, if you have access to robust government-sponsored coverage—certain military-related programs, for example—you shouldn't assume Marketplace discounts will be available.

This is one of those areas where the right move isn't to memorize a list; it's to treat government coverage as a flashing yellow light. If you or your spouse has any kind of non-Marketplace government health benefit, pause and confirm how it interacts with Marketplace financial help before you build a plan around subsidies.

Your tax household matters more than your living room

Marketplace financial help is tied to your *tax* household: the people you include on your federal income tax return. That sounds obvious until you picture real families.

A 62-year-old may be supporting an adult child in grad school. A divorced parent may have alternating-year dependency claims. A grandparent may be caring for a grandchild. These situations aren't rare. They can dramatically change the rules outcome because household size and who is considered "in the family" for tax purposes affect eligibility and the size of the discount.

A couple of practical implications:

- If someone can claim you as a dependent, your eligibility for Marketplace financial help may be affected. This comes up for young adults and sometimes for older parents.
- If you're married, filing status can matter. Many households assume they can file separately as a tax tactic; the Marketplace discount rules don't always play nicely with that instinct.

This is why "health insurance planning" and "tax planning" are the same activity during the years before Medicare. The Marketplace isn't asking about your feelings; it's asking how you will file.

The most expensive mistake: assuming job loss automatically means subsidy eligibility

When someone leaves a job—voluntarily or not—it feels like the system should smoothly move them into subsidized coverage. Sometimes it does. Sometimes it doesn't, and the difference is usually one of these:

- You (or your spouse) still have an offer of job-based coverage that meets the affordability/minimum-value tests.
- You're eligible for Medicare.
- You're eligible for Medicaid/CHIP.
- You're enrolled in other qualifying coverage for some or all months (including COBRA).

The sting is that this mistake often shows up only after you've done all the "responsible adult" steps: you retire, you apply, you pick a plan, you set up autopay. Then the numbers don't match what you expected, and your budget gets hit with a premium that feels like it was priced for a different household.

The cure is not obsessive rule-reading. It's a simple habit: identify possible blockers *first*, then shop.

A pre-shopping checklist that prevents nasty surprises

Before you spend a single minute comparing networks or debating Bronze versus Gold, run through these questions like a pilot's pre-flight:

1. *Will anyone in our tax household be eligible for Medicare at any point during the coverage year?* (Turning 65 is the obvious trigger, but other Medicare eligibility can exist too.)
2. *Does anyone have an offer of job-based coverage next year?* Include spouse coverage, part-time work with benefits, and any "you could enroll if you want" offers.
3. *If there is an employer offer, is it considered affordable and does it provide minimum value under the rules?* Don't guess based on your gut. If this is relevant, get the employer plan details and confirm.
4. *Are we currently enrolled in COBRA or planning to enroll?* If yes, decide whether COBRA is a temporary bridge or a full-year strategy, and understand the months it covers.
5. *Could our projected income put any household members in Medicaid/CHIP territory?* Especially in a year with unusually low income.
6. *Who exactly is in our tax household for the year?* Confirm dependency claims and expected filing status.

Notice what's missing: there's nothing here about "finding the cheapest plan." That's on purpose. Price comparisons only become meaningful after you know whether the Marketplace discount is even on the table.

Why this matters even if you're willing to pay full price

Some households shrug and say, "Fine. We'll just pay whatever it costs." That can be a rational choice, especially for people with high assets who want a particular network. But even then, these rules still matter because they affect your options and timing.

If you're blocked from financial help due to a spouse's employer offer, you might decide to join the spouse's plan, not because it's perfect, but because paying full price on the Marketplace is a bad deal. Or you might decide the opposite: keep the spouse plan for the working spouse and pay full price for a Marketplace plan for the retiree, because the network is worth it. The point is that you're making a conscious tradeoff instead of stumbling into one.

And if you *are* counting on financial help—which is common for households living on a carefully managed income—this eligibility gate is everything. It's the difference between a plan that fits neatly into the budget and a plan that forces you to pull from accounts you didn't want to touch yet.

A final, calming thought: "blocked" doesn't mean "stuck"

Finding a blocker can feel like the system is closing ranks against you. Usually it's just information. If employer coverage is blocking you, you still have coverage—just through a different channel. If Medicaid is available, you may have access to excellent coverage with low out-of-pocket costs. If Medicare is coming up, you're approaching the most stable coverage phase many Americans ever get.

The Marketplace is still valuable even when it doesn't come with discounts: it's a transparent menu, it's regulated, and it gives you choices you may not have in the employer world. But the money-saving part of the Marketplace works only when you're in the group it was designed to help. Confirm that first, and the rest of the planning gets dramatically less stressful.

2.2 Enrollment Timing, Open Enrollment, and Special Enrollment Periods

Marketplace coverage rewards people who treat dates like dollars. Pick the wrong start date and you can pay for an extra month of employer coverage you didn't need, or worse, end up with a clean spreadsheet and a dirty little uninsured gap right where you least want it. Pick the right start date and the whole transition into leaving work feels almost boring—which is the highest compliment you can give any insurance plan.

The trick is that Marketplace enrollment is not "whenever you feel like it." It runs on two clocks: a predictable annual window (open enrollment), and a set of trapdoors (special enrollment periods) that open only when something specific happens. Early retirement planning is mostly about deciding which clock you're going to use and then building your resignation date, your employer coverage end date, and your Marketplace effective date so they click into place.

Open enrollment: the calm, annual window

Open enrollment is the regular season. If nothing changes in your life and you simply want coverage for next year, this is the window that matters.

For plan year 2026 on HealthCare.gov, open enrollment ran from November 1, 2025 through January 15, 2026. There was also a split personality to the deadline: enrolling by December 15, 2025 enabled a January 1, 2026 effective date, while enrolling after December 15 and before January 15 could start February 1, 2026. That one-month slip is the kind of detail that can cost real money if you're timing a retirement around New Year's.

Two important qualifiers keep open enrollment from being as simple as it sounds:

- State-based Marketplaces can use different or extended deadlines. If you live in a state that runs its own Marketplace, treat dates you see on national news articles as a hint, not a promise. Verify your state's calendar before you anchor a retirement date to it.
- Policy changes can shift the calendar. CMS materials include a policy note that annual open enrollment timing changes starting plan year 2027. Even if you're reading this years later, take away the habit, not the specific dates: always confirm the current window for your Marketplace.

Open enrollment is the easiest way to enroll because you don't need to "prove" a life event. You just sign up. If you can plan your early retirement so your coverage transition happens neatly through open enrollment, you get fewer surprises and less paperwork.

Special enrollment periods: the trapdoors that make early retirement possible

Most people don't retire on November 1. They retire when the bonus hits, when the project ends, when the school year finishes, or when they simply can't do another Monday. That means open enrollment often isn't the right tool. Special enrollment periods (SEPs) are what let you enroll midyear when your life changes.

A SEP is permission to enroll or change plans outside the annual window because something significant happened—something the rules recognize as a legitimate reason to need coverage now rather than later.

The most important SEP for someone leaving work is the loss of job-based coverage. But "loss of coverage" has a specific feel to it: it's about losing *eligibility for the plan* or losing the plan itself, not about losing a job title. Quit your job but keep your employer coverage for three more months because you're paid through the end of the quarter? The SEP usually keys off the coverage ending, not your last day in the office.

The second big SEP category is moving—especially moves that change what plans are available. People underestimate how much the Marketplace is tied to geography. A move across state lines is almost always a different insurance universe.

Other SEPs exist too (marriage, divorce, having a child, gaining citizenship/lawful presence), but retirement planning tends to revolve around three: loss of job-based coverage, moving, and household changes.

Timing works backward: choose the last day of coverage first

A satisfying retirement plan reads like a calendar, not a wish:

> "What is the last day our current plan covers us? What is the first day we want the new plan to cover us? What action date makes those line up?"

Start with the last day of your employer coverage. This is not always your last day of work.

Employer coverage commonly ends in one of a few ways:

- Coverage ends on your last day of employment.
- Coverage ends at the end of the month you leave.
- Coverage continues through a severance period (sometimes treated as active coverage, sometimes not, depending on how it's administered).

HR can tell you which one applies in your case, and it's worth getting in writing. A one-sentence email confirming the coverage end date can prevent a month of confusion later.

Once you know the employer coverage end date, the goal is simple: Marketplace coverage effective the very next day (or the first of the following month, depending on rules and effective-date mechanics). If you're planning to use COBRA as a bridge, your "last day of coverage" might be the end of COBRA, not the end of active employment.

A concrete example: retire on June 30, coverage ends July 1

Suppose you retire on June 30 and your employer plan ends at midnight. July 1 is now a cliff: you're either covered by something else on July 1 or you're rolling the dice.

In this situation, a loss-of-coverage SEP is usually the cleanest tool. The retirement itself isn't the magic key; the end of your job-based coverage is. The practical steps are:

- Confirm the exact end date of employer coverage.
- Apply for Marketplace coverage using the SEP tied to losing coverage.
- Select a plan with an effective date that starts when employer coverage stops.

What makes this feel surprisingly intense is that you're doing paperwork at the same time you're doing life: exiting a job, saying goodbyes, turning in devices, maybe relocating or traveling. That's why it helps to treat the enrollment action like a scheduled appointment, not a background task you'll "get to."

The difference between "I can enroll" and "my plan starts"

Marketplace enrollment has two moments that people blur together:

- The day you submit the enrollment (your action date).
- The day coverage becomes effective (your coverage date).

Those dates can be weeks apart. That's not bureaucracy for its own sake; it's how insurers operate. They need a clean start date to set up premiums, cards, networks, and claims.

So when you plan your transition, don't just circle "retirement date." Circle the *coverage effective date* you need. Then back into the required enrollment action date, leaving extra time for decision-making, identity verification, and gathering documents if needed.

SEPs are real, but they're not vibes

A common frustration goes like this: "My situation changed. Obviously I need coverage. Why can't I just sign up?"

Because the Marketplace isn't trying to judge your need; it's trying to prevent gaming. Without rules, people could wait until they got sick to enroll, and the entire insurance pool would collapse. SEPs are the compromise: flexibility when life truly changes, but not unlimited flexibility.

That means some events that feel meaningful don't open a SEP by themselves. Examples that often *don't* create a SEP on their own include:

- Simply deciding you don't like your current plan.
- Voluntarily dropping coverage without another qualifying reason.
- Missing open enrollment and then feeling motivated in March.

This is why retirement timing can't be left to vibes either. If you're leaving work midyear and want a Marketplace plan right away, you need a qualifying event—typically the loss of job-based coverage—to legally open the enrollment door.

Moving: a SEP that can be either liberating or messy

Moves come in two flavors: the kind that simply changes your mailing address, and the kind that changes your entire set of plan options. The Marketplace cares about the second kind.

For someone retiring, moving can be part of the dream: downsize, relocate closer to family, try a different state, live near hiking trails, or follow a grandchild. But insurance networks are local creatures. A plan that's fantastic in one county can be useless in another.

If you move and gain access to different plans, you may qualify for a move-based SEP. Practically, that means you can switch plans outside open enrollment.

The messy part is proof and timing. Moves can be hard to document cleanly if you're between homes, using a mail service, living in an RV, or doing a "slow move" over months. If a move is part of the retirement plan, set yourself up with the kind of documentation that makes life easier: lease start dates, closing documents, utility bills—anything that makes your new residence real on paper.

Household changes: marriage, divorce, and new dependents

Insurance follows families the way tax rules do: sometimes imperfectly, always consequentially.

Marriage and divorce can trigger SEPs. So can having a baby or adopting a child. These events matter not just for enrollment access, but also because they can change household size and income expectations in ways that change affordability.

What retirement planning adds is awkward timing. A person might retire the same year they get divorced, or marry a partner with kids, or become the caregiver for a grandchild. These events are emotionally heavy; the last thing anyone wants is an enrollment problem on top. The practical move is to treat the SEP as part of the to-do list alongside the legal and financial paperwork, not as an afterthought.

COBRA vs. Marketplace: timing is often the real deciding factor

When someone leaves a job with benefits, the first fork in the road is often COBRA versus Marketplace coverage. People tend to focus on premiums and networks (fair), but timing often decides the case.

COBRA can be activated quickly and can keep you in the same network, which is valuable if you're mid-treatment or have doctors you refuse to give up. But COBRA can also become a "default extension" that drifts for months because it feels safe. If your long-term plan is a Marketplace policy, drifting has a cost: you can miss the cleanest windows to switch, and you might not notice until you're staring at an enrollment calendar that doesn't forgive late decisions.

Marketplace coverage, meanwhile, typically requires you to act within the SEP window and line up effective dates carefully. It's less forgiving but often more controllable for people who plan ahead—especially those who are managing income intentionally and want the monthly discount.

A good way to make the decision is to ask a timing-first question:

> "Do we need continuity tomorrow, or can we plan for a clean handoff on the first of a month?"

If you need continuity tomorrow, COBRA may be the simplest. If you can plan for a clean handoff, a Marketplace plan often fits well.

The "one-month gap" trap around New Year's

New Year's is when many people want to make changes: retire at year-end, simplify taxes, reset routines. Unfortunately, it's also where Marketplace effective dates can create a sneaky gap if you assume "enroll by January 15 means coverage starts January 1."

On HealthCare.gov for plan year 2026, enrolling by December 15, 2025 enabled a January 1 start. Enrolling after that could start February 1. The lived experience of this rule is simple: miss the earlier deadline and January might be uncovered unless you have another source of coverage for that month.

Even if your Marketplace uses different dates, the principle holds: there is often a "clean start" deadline that matters if you want coverage effective January 1. If retiring at year-end is part of your plan, anchor your calendar to the enrollment deadline that produces the January 1 effective date, not just the final day of open enrollment.

A planning table that fits on one page

When timing gets stressful, it's usually because the information is scattered: an HR PDF, a termination letter, an email chain, and a browser full of Marketplace tabs. Put the key dates into a single table and the anxiety drops.

Date/Item	*What you're confirming*
Last day of work	Your final day on payroll (may not equal coverage end date)
Employer plan coverage end date	The last day your job-based plan pays claims
COBRA election window	How long you have to elect COBRA (if considering it)
SEP trigger date	Usually the day coverage ends, move date, or household-change date
Marketplace application submitted	The day you file the application and select a plan
Marketplace effective date	The first day the new plan is active
First premium due / autopay set	The day you ensure the plan won't be cancelled for nonpayment

This isn't busywork. It's risk management with a calendar.

Documentation: the quiet reason people miss deadlines

A SEP is often simple in concept and annoying in execution. The most common speed bump is documentation—proof that the qualifying event happened.

If you're losing job-based coverage, you may be asked for something that confirms the coverage end date. If you're moving, you may be asked to show you moved. If your household changed, you may be asked for paperwork that supports it.

The practical strategy is to collect documents at the moment the event happens, when they're easiest to get. HR is more responsive while you're still employed. Closing documents are available at closing, not two months later when you're unpacking. Birth and adoption documents have their own timelines.

Think of documentation like a boarding pass: you can own the plane ticket (you qualify for a SEP), but you still need the pass to get through the gate.

State-based Marketplaces: don't assume your state plays by the same calendar

If your state runs its own Marketplace, you can't assume the HealthCare.gov calendar applies. Some state-based Marketplaces extend open enrollment, use slightly different effective-date rules, or have different processes for verifying SEPs. Consumer-facing guidance often emphasizes this for a reason: the differences are big enough to matter and common enough to trip up people who "did their research" on a national site.

The best habit is almost embarrassingly simple: when you start your enrollment plan, confirm (1) your state's open enrollment window, (2) how effective dates work for your enrollment date, and (3) the SEP rules most likely to apply to you.

How to choose a retirement date that makes insurance easy

People choose retirement dates for emotional and financial reasons: finish the year, hit a milestone birthday, vest in benefits, cash the bonus, avoid another winter commute. You can keep those priorities and still make insurance easier by adding one more filter: pick a date that produces a clean coverage transition.

Three patterns tend to produce fewer headaches:

- *End-of-month exits* when the employer plan ends at month-end, allowing a Marketplace plan to start on the first of the next month.
- *End-of-year exits* aligned with open enrollment deadlines that produce January 1 coverage.
- *Planned bridges* where COBRA is used intentionally for a defined period (for continuity of care), with a scheduled switch to Marketplace coverage using the appropriate enrollment window.

None of these are mandatory. They're just smoother. If you can make your retirement date land on a smooth pattern without sacrificing something important, you'll feel the benefit immediately.

A final operational habit: treat enrollment like a project, not an errand

An errand is something you do between other things. A project gets a due date, a dedicated hour on the calendar, and a folder where the documents live.

Marketplace enrollment deserves "project" status, because the downside of missing a deadline isn't inconvenience—it's exposure. Even a short uninsured stretch can turn a minor injury into a financial mess, and it can complicate later enrollment.

So give the process what it wants: a calendar, a coverage end date in writing, a decision deadline that's earlier than the official deadline, and a little respect for the fact that insurance is one of the few products in your life where "I'll do it next week" can be the most expensive sentence you say all year.

2.3 Metal Tiers, Silver Plans, and Cost-Sharing Reductions

A Marketplace plan is a little like a restaurant bill: the number that catches your eye first is the one at the top, but the real damage (or savings) happens in the fine print—what you pay when you actually use the thing you're buying. The metal tiers are the Marketplace's shortcut for that fine print. They're not "good, better, best." They're spending styles.

Marketplace plans are grouped into metal tiers intended to reflect average cost-sharing levels. In plain English, the tier is a rough promise about who tends to pay more over the year: you or the insurer. The tier doesn't tell you whether your favorite cardiologist is in-network or whether a certain brand-name drug is covered. But it does tell you whether the plan is built to be cheap *until something happens* or cheaper *when things happen*.

The best way to use metal tiers is to start with a brutally honest question: *What kind of year am I likely to have?* Not "What kind of year do I hope to have?" If you're 59, active, and rarely see a doctor, a low-premium plan can make sense. If you're 62 with ongoing physical therapy, expensive prescriptions, or a spouse who's been "keeping an eye on" a chronic condition, the premium is only the cover charge. The plan's real personality shows up at the pharmacy counter and the imaging desk.

The metal tiers are a cost-splitting deal, not a quality grade

Here's the core idea without the algebra: each metal tier represents how costs are typically split between the insurer and the insured across a broad population. The higher the metal, the more the plan tends to pay, on average, and the less you tend to pay when you use care. In exchange, you usually pay more each month.

That "on average" language matters. The tiers are about expected cost sharing across a standard mix of healthcare use. Your year might not be average. In fact, the whole point of insurance is that your year might be wildly un-average. So treat tiers like guardrails, not gospel.

A Bronze plan often has the lowest monthly price and the highest deductible, meaning you pay a lot out of pocket before the plan starts helping in a meaningful way. A Platinum plan is the opposite: you pay more each month, but you tend to face smaller bills when you need services. Silver and Gold sit in between.

One surprising twist: the tiers are not a perfect ladder. A particular Silver plan can have a higher deductible than a particular Bronze plan, and a Gold plan can have quirks that make it feel stingy for certain services. The tier is about the plan's overall design, not every individual line item.

Deductibles: the plan's "you're on your own" phase

Retirement is when many households become more sensitive to deductibles, not less. When you're working, a $3,000 deductible is painful but sometimes absorbed by cash flow. When you're living off investments and managing taxable income carefully, a $3,000 surprise can force a sale you didn't want to make.

A deductible is the amount you generally pay for covered services before the plan starts paying (with plenty of exceptions and fine print, especially for preventive care). Think of it as the plan's "prove you're serious" threshold.

Bronze plans are often built around a high deductible. That's not inherently bad. It's a design choice: keep the premium low and use the deductible as the main way to keep costs down for the insurer. For a genuinely low-utilization household, this can be efficient. But households frequently misunderstand what "low utilization" means.

If you have:

- a few specialist visits,
- a round of physical therapy,
- an MRI,
- ongoing prescriptions,

you can chew through a deductible faster than you expect. That's when Bronze stops feeling like a bargain and starts feeling like a monthly membership fee that still charges admission.

Copays and coinsurance: the plan's personality once the deductible is met

After the deductible phase, plans tend to shift to copays (fixed dollar amounts) or coinsurance (a percentage of the cost). This is where tiers can feel very different in daily life.

A Gold plan often looks like a "normal" employer plan to people who are used to working coverage: reasonable copays for office visits, more predictable costs for common services, and fewer moments where you stare at a bill and wonder if it has a typo.

Bronze plans often lean hard on coinsurance after the deductible, which can make costs feel opaque. Coinsurance is fine when the underlying negotiated prices are low; it is less fine when you're dealing with hospital facilities, imaging centers, or specialty drugs where the sticker shock arrives disguised as "20%."

This is why shoppers who focus only on the monthly premium sometimes end up unhappy. The plan that saved you $300/month can cost you $2,000 in an unlucky spring.

Metal tiers are really about risk tolerance

A helpful way to frame the tier decision is as a choice between two kinds of discomfort:

- *Premium discomfort*: paying more every month, even when you barely use care.
- *Bill discomfort*: paying less every month, but accepting the possibility of large bills when you need services.

Some people hate premium discomfort. They want the lowest fixed expense, and they're willing to self-insure routine care with savings. Others hate bill discomfort. They would rather pay a higher premium and sleep better knowing that an ER visit won't trigger a financial scramble.

Neither preference is "right." What matters is matching the tier to the reality of your health and your finances. If your budget can absorb a $6,000 surprise without selling investments at a bad time, a lower premium plan becomes more viable. If a large surprise would force a withdrawal you were trying to avoid, paying more in premiums can be a form of financial smoothing.

Why Silver is not "the middle option" for many households

Silver sounds like the compromise tier: not cheap, not premium. But Silver has a special feature that breaks the neat ladder: Cost-Sharing Reductions (CSRs).

Cost-Sharing Reductions lower deductibles, copays, and coinsurance, but only apply if the enrollee selects a Silver plan. That's the key sentence. It's not "CSR helps you pick a better plan." It's "CSR changes what a Silver plan *is*."

Policy descriptions explain CSR in terms of actuarial value—the percentage of costs the plan is expected to cover for a standard population. Without turning this into a statistics lecture, here's the practical punchline: CSR requires insurers to offer Silver plan variations with higher actuarial values (73%, 87%, 94%) for eligible income ranges (generally 100%–250% FPL). In everyday language, that means a Silver plan can quietly behave like a Gold or even Platinum plan in terms of what you pay when you use care.

If your household is eligible for CSR and you pick Silver, you're not buying "Silver." You're buying "Silver with turbochargers." If you pick Bronze or Gold, you don't get CSR at all, even if your income would have qualified. This is why some shoppers end up in a daze: they see a Bronze premium that looks irresistible, but they don't realize they're giving up a hidden upgrade that would have reduced their deductible and copays dramatically.

CSR is about usage, not virtue

CSR is sometimes misunderstood as a reward for buying a "responsible" plan. It's not. It's an affordability tool that targets out-of-pocket costs for lower-income households. The Marketplace discount that reduces premiums helps you get in the door; CSR helps you pay for what happens once you're inside.

That's also why CSR matters so much for people who are healthy until they're not. You don't need CSR for routine preventive care if you rarely use services. You need it when a year turns complicated: a new diagnosis, a surgery, a string of specialist visits, a medication that suddenly becomes non-optional.

A Silver plan with CSR can turn those moments from financially destabilizing to merely annoying. It's the difference between "we can handle this" and "we need to rethink everything."

A tale of two Silvers: how the same tier can feel like two different products

Two households can both say, "We have a Silver plan," and mean completely different things.

Household A selects a standard Silver plan with no CSR. Their deductible and coinsurance look like what most people expect from a mid-tier plan.

Household B selects a Silver plan with CSR. Their deductible might be dramatically lower, copays may be more generous, and the plan may start paying meaningful portions of costs sooner.

Both are "Silver." Only one is *Silver-with-CSR*, and the difference shows up the first time you need imaging or an outpatient procedure.

This is why it's dangerous to take advice from a neighbor who has "the same tier." Unless you know whether CSR is involved, you're not comparing like with like.

The premium twist: Silver loading can make Gold look oddly cheap

Marketplace pricing contains a strange but useful quirk often referred to as *silver loading*. The short version: in many places, the way CSR is financed has caused insurers to load extra costs into the premiums of Silver plans. The result can be counterintuitive after subsidies are applied: Gold plans can end up relatively inexpensive for households receiving the monthly discount, sometimes even close to (or below) the net premium of Silver.

This creates a second "Silver isn't the middle" effect:

- If you qualify for CSR, Silver is special because it unlocks better cost sharing.
- If you do *not* qualify for CSR but you do receive a premium subsidy, Gold can become the value tier because the subsidy

is pegged to a Silver benchmark while Silver premiums may be inflated by silver loading.

That's not a loophole so much as a market dynamic. But it does mean you should shop with curiosity rather than assumptions. The label on the plan might say Gold, but the price tag might say "why is this not everyone's default?"

One caution: none of this means you should blindly chase Gold. Networks, drug formularies, and plan rules still matter. It simply means the metal ladder can warp in the presence of subsidies and silver loading. If you never look at Gold because you assume it must cost more, you can miss a deal that exists specifically because of how the system is wired.

Bronze: the plan that works beautifully until it doesn't

Bronze has a loyal fan club for a reason. It can be the right tool for:

- people with very low expected use,
- people with significant savings who can absorb a bad year,
- people who care most about keeping fixed monthly expenses low,
- people using the plan primarily as catastrophic coverage.

The failure mode is also predictable: you pick Bronze thinking "I'm healthy," and then you discover that your expected use wasn't low; it was merely *unknown*. A new prescription, a couple of specialist referrals, and a surprise outpatient procedure can turn Bronze into a plan where you pay almost everything yourself, just with the insurer negotiating the prices.

Bronze can still be a rational choice—even a savvy one—if you make it deliberately and you have the liquidity to handle the deductible without tearing up your financial plan.

Platinum: the "high premium, low drama" tier (when available)

Platinum plans aren't available everywhere, and when they are, they're often priced for people who know they will use significant care. In the right situation, Platinum can feel like buying peace: more predictable copays, less deductible pain, and fewer "wait, how much?" moments.

But Platinum is not automatically the best option for someone in their early 60s. Premiums can be high, and if your actual use is low, you may be paying for a level of protection you don't need. Platinum is at its best when you have known, ongoing utilization and you want to reduce variability. It's less compelling as a defensive purchase if your budget is tight or if you're mainly trying to control monthly costs.

How to shop tiers like a retiree, not like a shopper

When you buy a toaster, you can compare features and reviews and feel done. When you buy a Marketplace plan, you're buying a contract about how you'll split uncertain future costs. That's why the "right" tier isn't a moral choice; it's a forecast plus a risk preference.

A practical shopping approach looks like this:

1. *Write down your "likely year" and your "bad year."* Likely year might be a few prescriptions and routine visits. Bad year might include an ER visit, imaging, surgery, or a new chronic medication.
2. *For each plan you're considering, identify the costs that would hit you in the bad year.* Don't stop at the deductible. Look for specialist copays/coinsurance, imaging rules, and how quickly costs accumulate.
3. *If you are eligible for CSR, treat Silver as the default until another plan clearly beats it for your situation.* Not because Silver is "best," but because CSR can make it a different animal.

4. *If you are not eligible for CSR but you receive premium subsidies, check Gold anyway.* Silver loading can create weird bargains. Weird bargains are still bargains.

Notice the theme: you're shopping for *total financial behavior*, not for a tier label.

The quiet deal-breakers that tiers don't capture

Two plans can share the same metal tier and still feel like they come from different planets. That's because the tier doesn't capture:

- *Network quality*: whether your doctors and hospitals are in-network.
- *Drug coverage*: whether your medications are covered and under what cost-sharing.
- *Service rules*: referrals, prior authorization, and whether the plan is HMO/EPO/PPO-style.

So use metal tiers to narrow the field, then do the unglamorous work: check your doctors, check your drugs, and sanity-check the plan's cost sharing for the services you're most likely to use.

A closing mindset that pays off

Metal tiers are the Marketplace's way of saying, "Pick your style of paying." Silver with CSR is the system whispering, "If you qualify, don't ignore this." And silver loading is the system's accidental prank that can sometimes put a Gold plan on sale.

If you take one habit from all of this, make it this: don't let the premium be the main character. Let the plan's behavior over a real year—especially a messy year—be the deciding factor. That's how you pick coverage that supports your retirement instead of threatening it.

2.4 Premium Tax Credits and the Logic Behind Subsidies

The Marketplace discount works less like a coupon and more like a price-matching guarantee. Not against Amazon or Costco—against a reference plan the law uses as a yardstick. If your household income sits in the range the rules target, the government effectively says: *"You shouldn't have to spend more than about this much on a standard plan in your area."* The rest is filled in with a tax credit.

That framing clears up a lot of confusion. People assume the subsidy is a mysterious number that pops out of a government computer. It's actually the result of two ideas that are easy to hold in your head at the same time:

- A benchmark plan sets the sticker price the system reacts to.
- An "expected contribution" sets what the household is supposed to pay, based on income.

The tax credit is the bridge between those two.

The benchmark: the plan you may never buy, but can't ignore

The tax credit is anchored to the benchmark (second-lowest-cost silver plan) premium in the enrollee's area minus the household's expected contribution on a sliding scale. The benchmark is a real plan with a real premium in your county/ZIP—but it's not necessarily the plan you should enroll in, and many people don't.

That's the first counterintuitive point: the benchmark is like the "reference car" in a safety rating. You might drive something else. The system still needs a consistent yardstick.

Because it's tied to your location, the benchmark makes the Marketplace intensely local. Two couples with the same age, same income, same everything—living in different counties—can see very different credits simply because the benchmark premium is different where they live. It's not favoritism; it's math reacting to local pricing.

Expected contribution: a sliding scale that turns income into a target premium

The second ingredient is the expected contribution. This is the part that makes the subsidy feel "means-tested" without asking about your net worth. The law looks at household income as a percent of the federal poverty level (FPL) and assigns an expected share of income you're supposed to pay toward the benchmark.

You don't need to memorize the table of percentages to plan well. What you need is the shape of the relationship:

- At lower incomes, the expected contribution is smaller, so the credit tends to be larger.
- As income rises, the expected contribution rises, shrinking the credit.

A useful way to think about it is elastic: as your income stretches upward, your "required share" stretches too.

The credit is the gap: benchmark premium minus expected contribution

Once you have those two pieces, the logic becomes almost disappointingly simple:

> *Tax credit = benchmark premium – expected household contribution*

If the benchmark premium is high in your area, the gap tends to be larger. If your income is higher (so your expected contribution is higher), the gap tends to be smaller.

That's why two people can talk past each other even if they're both "in the Marketplace." One person says, "We pay almost nothing for premiums." Another says, "We get basically no help." Both can be telling the truth, depending on income and local benchmark pricing.

A credit you can use on (almost) any metal tier

Here's a practical feature that feels like a loophole the first time you hear it: the premium tax credit can generally be applied to any Marketplace metal plan (Bronze/Silver/Gold/Platinum), even though it is computed from the benchmark Silver premium.

That means the benchmark is a measuring stick, not a shackle. You can take the credit and "spend" it on a Bronze plan with a lower sticker price, potentially driving your net premium very low. Or you can apply it to a Gold plan, using the credit to buy richer coverage with better cost-sharing.

This flexibility is why the Marketplace can be unusually strategic for people who plan their income. The credit isn't tied to your plan choice; it's tied to your income and the benchmark where you live.

One nuance worth holding onto: while the credit can be used across metal levels, cost-sharing reductions (CSRs) are a separate benefit and only attach to Silver plans. So even though you can apply the credit to Gold, you can't "carry" CSR with you. (You don't need to re-learn CSR here—just remember it's a separate lever with a Silver-only lock.)

Advance payments: the monthly discount is a prepayment of a tax benefit

Consumers can take the credit in advance (APTC) to lower monthly premiums, which must later be reconciled on the tax return. In everyday life, "advance" means you're choosing between two cash-flow styles:

- *Take it monthly*: lower premiums now, smaller credit (or possible payback) later.
- *Take it at tax time*: pay more each month, then claim the credit on your return.

Most households use the monthly version because it's hard to float large premiums for a year just to get reimbursed later. But it's still a choice, and it's worth recognizing it as one. If your income is volatile and you hate surprises at filing time, you may prefer to take less in advance and settle up later. If your cash flow is tight, taking it in advance can make coverage possible.

Either way, the underlying credit is the same; the timing is different.

Household size: the quiet multiplier in the background

Household size affects two things at once:

- Your FPL baseline (the denominator in "income as a percent of FPL").
- The benchmark premium you're matching against (two 60-year-olds cost more than one 60-year-old).

That's why "same income" doesn't mean "same subsidy."

A single 62-year-old and a married couple at the same income can land in very different places on the subsidy scale. The couple's income may be a lower percent of FPL because the poverty guideline for two people is higher. At the same time, their benchmark premium may be higher because they're buying coverage for two. The system is balancing these forces.

It's also why dependency decisions—who is in your tax household—can ripple into affordability in ways that don't feel intuitive. Adding someone to the tax household changes the FPL comparison and can shift the expected contribution rate, but it may also change the cost of the benchmark coverage you're pricing against.

Geography: why the same income can buy different affordability

It can feel unfair that your county matters so much. But insurance pricing is intensely tied to local provider markets, competition among insurers, and regional healthcare costs. The Marketplace doesn't flatten that; it reacts to it.

The important planning lesson is practical, not philosophical: if you're considering a move in retirement—especially across state lines—treat "benchmark premium in the new location" as a real planning input. The move may improve your taxes, your housing costs, and your lifestyle, yet make coverage more expensive (or the reverse). That's not a reason not to move; it's a reason to check before you commit.

A simple numerical story (without turning it into homework)

Imagine the benchmark premium for your area is $1,200/month for your household.

Now imagine the expected contribution for your income works out to $300/month.

The math is then:

> $1,200 (benchmark) – $300 (expected contribution) = $900/month credit

You can apply that $900/month to other plans too. If a Bronze plan costs $900/month, your net premium could be near $0. If a Gold plan costs $1,350/month, your net premium might be $450/month.

Notice what that does psychologically. Instead of thinking "Bronze is $900 and Gold is $1,350," you think "Bronze is almost free and Gold is $450." Same plans, different reality—because the credit is doing its job in the background.

Also notice what you *can't* do with the credit: you can't take more credit than the premium you owe for the plan you pick. In other words, the credit can reduce your premium down to zero, but it generally doesn't turn your insurance policy into a cash rebate.

Why subsidy rules can feel like shifting sand

Even if the core mechanism stays the same, policy can change the boundaries. CMS overview notes recent policy context: ARP expanded subsidies above 400% FPL for 2021—2022 and IRA extended through plan year 2025. For planning, the key takeaway isn't to memorize acronyms; it's to adopt a cautious posture:

- The benchmark/expected-contribution framework is the engine.
- The exact generosity of the engine—and where it phases out—can be adjusted by legislation.

So it's wise to treat "what happens at higher incomes" as a rule that may change over time, and to re-check assumptions each year you enroll. People get into trouble by building a multi-year plan on a one-year subsidy landscape.

The "why" behind the design: keeping insurance from becoming a luxury good

There's a reason the system uses a benchmark and an income-based contribution rather than simply giving everyone a flat-dollar subsidy. A flat subsidy would help some households too much and others not enough, because premiums vary dramatically by age and geography. Anchoring the credit to the benchmark makes it responsive to local premium levels, while expected contribution ties affordability to ability to pay.

That's also why the credit is a tax credit rather than a direct price control. Insurers still set premiums. The government is stepping in on the buyer's side to keep coverage within reach—at least for households that fit the eligibility rules.

Planning with the logic: what you can predict before you shop

Once you understand the moving pieces, you can make your plan search feel less like scrolling and more like modeling:

- If you anticipate lower income (as a percent of FPL), expect a larger credit and lower net premiums—especially for the benchmark.
- If you anticipate a move to a more expensive rating area, expect the benchmark premium to rise, which can increase the credit—but not always enough to fully offset the higher sticker prices across plans.
- If your household size changes, don't assume the effect is one-directional. It can change both your percent-of-FPL and the cost of the benchmark plan.
- If you plan to choose a non-benchmark plan (Bronze or Gold), remember the credit follows you; you're not "stuck" buying Silver simply because the benchmark is Silver.

This is where Marketplace shopping becomes oddly empowering. Instead of asking, "What will the website offer me?" you start asking, "If our income lands here, what range of net premiums is plausible?"

A line you can hold in your head: net premiums tend to rise as income rises

The relationship between income (as a percent of FPL) and net premium cost is not perfectly smooth in real life. It's shaped by local premiums, household composition, and the year's rules. But as a general mental model, higher income tends to mean a higher expected contribution and therefore higher net premiums.

Near the end of this discussion is a simple chart that captures that intuition. It's intentionally not precise to any single year's table or any single county's benchmark. It's meant to show the *behavior* of the system: net premium burden typically grows as income rises, and it often changes more noticeably around key ranges.

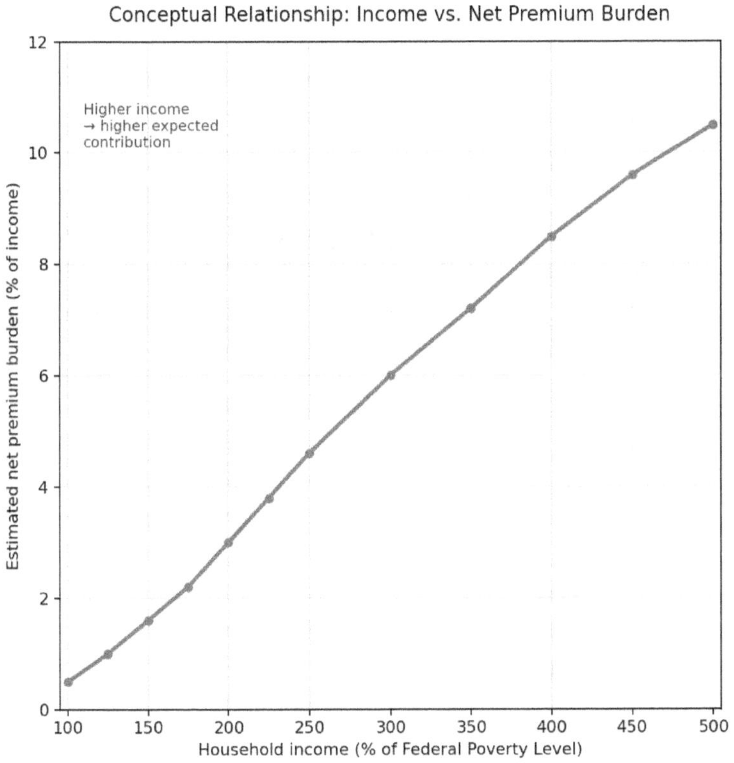

The practical payoff: fewer surprises, better choices

Once you see the benchmark-and-expected-contribution logic, a lot of Marketplace behavior stops feeling personal. If your net premium jumps after you realize more income than planned, it isn't the site "taking away" help—it's the expected contribution rising and shrinking the credit. If your friend in another county gets a bigger credit at the same income, it's not luck—it's a different benchmark premium. If a Gold plan sometimes looks like it's been put on sale, it's often because the credit is computed from Silver and can be applied broadly.

That predictability is the real gift. Not because it guarantees low costs—nothing in U.S. medical care does that—but because it turns what looks like a black box into a set of levers you can plan around.

2.5 Reconciliation, Payback Risk, and the Subsidy Cliff Mindset

The Marketplace discount has a personality trait that is both generous and slightly unnerving: it pays you based on what you *predict,* then settles up based on what actually happened. That's why a year of coverage can end with an unexpected invoice—or an unexpected extra benefit—right when you thought the story was over.

The unsettling part isn't that the rules are cruel. It's that retirement income is often lumpy in ways W-2 life never prepared you for. A bonus doesn't happen anymore, but a mutual fund can throw off a surprise distribution. A one-time IRA withdrawal becomes a "small" conversion that grows as you add withholding. A house sale can land in the same calendar year as a portfolio rebalance. You're not being reckless; you're living a normal financial life with irregular inputs. The reconciliation process is where those irregularities show up.

Reconciliation: the moment the estimate becomes real

Advance subsidies are just that—advance. APTC is an advance estimate; Form 8962 reconciles APTC against the PTC actually allowed based on final household income and family circumstances. Translating that into everyday English:

> You told the Marketplace what you expected your income and household would be. The government helped during the year based on that estimate. At tax time, you run the true numbers and reconcile the help you received with the help you were entitled to.

Reconciliation is not an audit. It's bookkeeping. The Marketplace front-loads affordability by paying part of your premium during the year, and the tax return is where the system checks whether the advance payments matched reality.

This is why the monthly discount should never be treated as "free money." It's conditional. If your year goes sideways in the direction of higher income, part of that discount can reverse.

The one form you can't ignore: 1095-A

The reconciliation starts with a piece of paper (or a PDF) most people don't even know exists until January: Form 1095-A. Form 1095-A is the key Marketplace document used to reconcile premiums and APTC; failure to reconcile can delay refunds and may affect future APTC eligibility.

Think of 1095-A as the Marketplace's version of a W-2. It tells you, month by month, what plan you had, what the benchmark premium was for that month, and how much advance subsidy was paid on your behalf. You don't need to understand every box to appreciate the stakes: the numbers on that form flow into Form 8962, and Form 8962 flows into your tax return.

If you or your preparer files without reconciling, the IRS won't shrug. Refunds can be delayed, and you can create problems for yourself the following year. The Marketplace is happy to reduce your premiums up front, but it expects you to close the loop.

Form 8962: where the year's story gets rewritten

Form 8962 is where your year becomes a single verdict: did you receive too much APTC, too little, or just right?

The form compares:

- what you *received* in advance payments during the year, and

- what you were *allowed* based on final household income and household composition.

If you were allowed more than you received, you get an additional credit on your return. If you received more than you were allowed, you repay some or all of the excess.

This is where the emotional sting often happens. People experience repayment as a punishment, even though it's simply the system correcting an estimate. But emotionally, it can still land like a surprise bill for being "wrong about retirement."

Why early retirement income makes reconciliation more dramatic

W-2 households have income that's relatively stable and relatively visible. Retired households often have income that is:

- easier to change late in the year,
- partially driven by markets, and
- influenced by tax decisions you control (timing sales, conversions, withdrawals).

That combination is exactly what makes the Marketplace powerful for planners—and exactly what makes reconciliation risky for improvisers.

A mid-year raise doesn't exist anymore, but a mid-year market rally does. A cash cushion can reduce the need for taxable withdrawals, but a home repair can increase it. A retiree can decide in December to convert more (or less) from an IRA, and that single decision can swing the final income number enough to change the allowed subsidy.

You don't need to fear this. You need to respect it.

Payback risk: the "too much help" problem

Payback happens when your final income ends up higher than what you told the Marketplace, and the higher income means you were entitled to less assistance than you received.

The most common triggers are not exotic. They're the kinds of things people do to run a good retirement:

- Selling appreciated investments to rebalance or raise cash.
- Unplanned taxable distributions from mutual funds.
- Part-time or consulting work that grows beyond "just a little."
- A large year-end IRA conversion that seemed smart for long-term tax planning.

The pain point is that the Marketplace discount shows up as lower monthly premiums—quietly, incrementally—while the payback shows up as one loud number on the tax return. Psychologically, it feels like the government is taking something away. Mechanically, it's simply reconciling an estimate.

The 400% FPL line: why the "cliff mindset" still matters

Even in years when laws soften the worst edges, it's wise to keep a "cliff mindset." Not because you should panic, but because thresholds are where planning mistakes become expensive.

One specific rule is worth stating plainly because it's so consequential: repayment limitation mechanics depend on household income as a percent of FPL; the Form 8962 instructions explicitly state that at 400% FPL or more, there is no repayment limitation (full repayment of excess APTC).

That sentence has teeth. It means that if your income ends up at or above that line (under rules where that line applies), any excess advance payments may be fully repayable. No gentle cap. No partial forgiveness. Just a full true-up.

This is the source of the "subsidy cliff" anxiety people talk about, and it explains why retirees who are otherwise calm about taxes can become laser-focused about income thresholds. The issue isn't a moral failing; it's the asymmetry between the ease of receiving APTC and the suddenness of paying it back.

It's also why seemingly benign end-of-year moves can be costly. A conversion you do on December 28 doesn't just add tax. It can retroactively reduce the allowable subsidy for the entire year, turning a tax-planning win into a cash-flow loss.

A defensive habit: treat your income estimate like a living document

Many households set their Marketplace income estimate once, at enrollment, and then never touch it. That's understandable—retirement already comes with a to-do list. But it's also how surprises grow.

Updating your estimate during the year is like steering a boat with small corrections rather than one dramatic turn at the end. If you realize in July that dividends and distributions are higher than expected, or that consulting income is real income now, you can update the Marketplace estimate so the monthly discount adjusts. That doesn't eliminate reconciliation. It reduces the odds of a nasty one-time payback.

This habit also changes your psychology. Instead of "wait and see what happens at tax time," you adopt "keep it roughly aligned as the year unfolds." The system was built for that.

Another defensive habit: build an income guardrail, not a single target

Retirees love targets: "We'll keep our income at $X." The Marketplace works better with guardrails: "We'll stay under *about* $X unless there's a compelling reason not to."

A single target fails because it assumes the year will cooperate. Guardrails acknowledge volatility. They also give you a decision rule: if you're approaching the upper rail, you pause before doing optional income actions.

Optional actions in retirement are the ones that tend to blow up reconciliation:

- elective conversions,
- elective investment sales,
- elective extra withdrawals for big purchases.

A guardrail turns those choices into conscious tradeoffs. You can still do them. You just do them with full awareness of the after-tax and after-subsidy cost.

The classic trap: the year-end conversion that looked "small"

Here's a very common storyline.

You're retired. Income is lower than during your working years. You decide to convert a chunk of pre-tax IRA money to Roth near year-end. You've run the tax brackets and you're thrilled: "We're filling the 12% bracket" or "We're staying under the next IRMAA tier." It looks like great planning.

Then tax season arrives and Form 8962 quietly informs you that your allowable subsidy was smaller than what you received. The payback effectively adds another marginal cost on top of the tax you planned for. The conversion wasn't "taxed at 12%." It was taxed at 12% plus whatever subsidy you had to give back.

This is not an argument against conversions. It's an argument against doing them blind to the healthcare side of the ledger. As we saw earlier, the Marketplace is lever-rich. That richness is a gift, but it comes with interactions.

What about the opposite case: income lower than expected?

Reconciliation isn't only about payback. If your final income ends up lower than projected, you may have been entitled to more assistance than you received during the year. In that case, Form 8962 can produce an additional credit on your tax return.

This can happen if:

- markets fell and you realized fewer taxable gains than expected,
- you delayed optional income actions,
- part-time work didn't materialize,
- you had unexpected deductions that lowered taxable income (within the rules).

The psychological trap here is the reverse: some people intentionally take very little advance help because they fear payback, and then they struggle with premiums all year only to discover they could have taken more in advance. There's no single "right" approach. But if cash flow matters, and your income estimate is reasonable, taking APTC in advance is often the point of the program.

A paperwork detail that becomes a strategy: monthly granularity

Marketplace subsidies and reconciliation are month-by-month under the hood. Your Form 1095-A reports premiums and advance payments by month. That matters because life changes don't happen neatly on January 1.

If you start coverage mid-year, switch plans, add a spouse, or move, your year may be a quilt of different months with different premiums and different advance payments. The reconciliation is designed to handle that complexity, but it means your recordkeeping has to be decent.

Practical tips that sound boring until they save you:

- Keep each year's 1095-A with your tax documents immediately when it arrives.
- Save eligibility notices and confirmation pages when you update income or household status.
- If you change plans mid-year, keep both sets of documents. The IRS won't intuit what happened; it will reconcile what was reported.

The goal isn't to become a filing cabinet enthusiast. It's to avoid the "I swear we paid that" conversation in March.

The emotional budgeting move: reserve a reconciliation buffer

Even with good planning, income can move. Markets move. Life moves. One of the most calming things you can do is create a small "reconciliation buffer" in your budget—a cash reserve earmarked for a possible payback.

This is especially useful in the first year after leaving work, when you're still learning what your retirement income looks like in practice. A buffer turns a potential April problem into a manageable adjustment. If no payback occurs, the buffer becomes next year's buffer, or it funds something fun. Either way, it reduces stress.

The buffer doesn't need to be huge to be effective. The point is to remove the sense that you're one tax form away from panic.

A practical way to think about the cliff mindset

The "cliff" metaphor makes people imagine falling off a ledge. The healthier mindset is more like driving in the mountains: the road has sharp turns, and you don't want to take them at 60 mph.

Sharp turns in Marketplace planning are the places where a small income change produces a big change in assistance, or where repayment caps disappear. You don't need to fear the road. You just slow down near the turns:

- Update income estimates when reality changes.
- Avoid optional income spikes late in the year unless you've run the numbers.
- Keep a cushion for the unknown.

That's defensive driving, not paranoia.

The payoff: the cheapest premium is only cheap after taxes

Marketplace coverage can look stunningly affordable in the moment—especially when the monthly discount is applied. The real test is whether it stays affordable after the year is reconciled.

Once you internalize that, your planning becomes calmer and more professional. You stop treating the monthly discount as a prize you "won," and you start treating it as a provisional number you manage. You don't avoid income. You sequence it thoughtfully. And you don't get blindsided by April.

Form 8962 isn't a villain. It's the receipt. The goal is to make sure the receipt matches the meal you intended to order.

Chapter 3

MAGI Management and Income Engineering

In early retirement, the biggest healthcare surprise is often not the premium itself, but the income number quietly driving it behind the scenes. This chapter shows how to treat MAGI less like a tax form mystery and more like a thermostat: something you can monitor, adjust, and use to keep both cash flow and coverage working together.

3.1 Tax Return Basics for ACA Planning

Health coverage in the gap years has a strange referee: not your budget, not your doctor, not even the insurance company. The referee is your tax filing. The dollars of assistance that make an individual policy affordable are calculated from the same set of definitions the IRS uses to decide who is in your household and what counts as income. That sounds intimidating until you realize the IRS is actually very consistent—just not always intuitive.

The mental shift that saves people real money is this: the subsidy system doesn't care who shares a fridge; it cares who shares a *tax return*. If a family member isn't part of your tax household, their income generally doesn't follow them onto your subsidy calculation. If they *are* part of your tax household, their income may count even if they're "just" a teen with a summer job. The rules are not about fairness or family dynamics. They're about forms.

The Tax Household: Your Real ACA "Household"

A tax household is the group of people whose names and Social Security numbers live together on one federal return. That's the unit used to measure income for financial help. It usually includes:

- The taxpayer(s): you, and your spouse if you file a joint return.
- Any dependents you claim on that return.

This sounds straightforward until real life shows up. Adult kids move back home. A parent lives with you. A fiancé shares expenses. A college student is away nine months of the year. The Marketplace application will ask who needs coverage, but the income calculation ultimately follows the tax household logic. Two homes can have identical people at the dinner table and completely different income counting rules depending on who claims whom.

Here's the practical planning move: before you even think about income strategies, confirm who will be on the return for the year you're buying coverage. Not who *should* be, not who *used to be*, but who you will actually claim.

Filing Status: The Switch That Can Change the Math

Your filing status is the label at the top of the return that tells the IRS what rulebook you're using: married filing jointly, single, head of household, and so on. For health-plan assistance, filing status matters because it can change eligibility and whose income is included.

Married filing jointly is the default for most married couples, and it typically keeps your options broad. For ACA assistance, the joint return merges two people into one tax household with one income number. That can be good (one spouse's lower income can soften the other's higher income), or it can be inconvenient (one spouse's large distribution can erase assistance for both).

Married filing separately is where people stumble. Many couples try it for non-health reasons—student loan plans, separation logistics, or a long-standing preference for "keeping things separate." But financial help for ACA coverage is generally not available to married taxpayers filing separately (with limited exceptions). In plain language: if you want the help, plan around a joint return unless you have a specific reason and have verified the consequences.

Head of household can be a powerful status for unmarried taxpayers supporting a dependent. It can also be a trap if assumed casually. The key ACA planning angle isn't the tax rates; it's that claiming a dependent brings another person into your tax household. That can change both the household size used for subsidy calculations and whether the dependent's income needs to be counted.

Dependents: Where "Whose Income Counts" Gets Weird

Claiming someone as a dependent does two things at once: it increases household size and can also pull in their income. Most people notice the first part and miss the second.

The assistance formula uses household income, and household income includes the modified adjusted gross income (ACA MAGI) of:

- the taxpayer,
- the spouse (if filing jointly), and
- dependents *who are required to file their own return.*

That last clause is the sneaky one. It doesn't say "dependents who have any income." It says dependents who *must file*. Many dependents have a small amount of earnings and either don't need to file or could file but aren't required. If they aren't required to file, their income generally doesn't enter the household income number for subsidy purposes, even though they're in your household size.

So the planning question is not "Does my teenager have a job?" It's "Does my teenager's income trigger a filing requirement?" In some years, a dependent's income is harmless background noise; in other years, it's the difference between qualifying for help and paying full freight.

This also explains a common surprise in early retirement households: the dependent you claim may be the one person in the house whose income is *most* likely to create a subsidy headache, because their income can jump in unpredictable ways (internships, a year of full-time work between school and grad school, a taxable scholarship piece, gig work). If you're managing your income carefully, you want that possibility on your radar early, not during tax filing season.

The Marketplace Application vs. the IRS: Who Wins?

The Marketplace asks you to estimate income for the year. That estimate is used to decide how much advance help to send to your insurer each month. It's a real cash-flow difference: the premium you pay can drop immediately.

But the IRS is the scorekeeper at year-end. The final amount of help you were *entitled* to is computed on the federal return using the actual household income for that year. If the advance payments were too high, you may have to repay some or all of the excess. If the advance payments were too low, you may get additional credit.

This creates a subtle incentive problem: the Marketplace wants a good-faith estimate; the IRS demands precision. For planning, that means you should treat your income estimate as a living number. If your year changes—a consulting project appears, a spouse returns to work, a large capital gain happens—the right move is often to update the estimate rather than hoping it all "comes out in the wash." The wash can be expensive.

AGI: The One Number Worth Memorizing

Adjusted gross income (AGI) is the backbone of the return. It's not your wages, not your total deposits, not your net worth. It's a line item that sits near the bottom of the "income" portion of Form 1040 after certain deductions called adjustments have been subtracted.

AGI matters here because ACA MAGI starts with AGI. If you know where AGI lives and what moves it up and down, you're 80% of the way to understanding your subsidy eligibility. The rest is a small set of add-backs.

A helpful way to think about AGI is as your "taxable-story income." It's the IRS's version of the year's narrative:

- Paychecks and self-employment profit are in the story.
- Interest and dividends are in the story.
- Capital gains are in the story (even if taxed at special rates).
- Traditional IRA distributions are in the story.
- A Roth IRA qualified withdrawal often isn't in the story at all.

Early retirees sometimes assume that because they're "not working," they have "no income." The IRS is unimpressed by that framing. Selling appreciated stock to fund groceries is income in the IRS narrative. Converting money from a traditional IRA to a Roth IRA is income in the IRS narrative. Taking a pension is income in the IRS narrative. AGI is where that narrative gets totaled.

ACA MAGI: Not a New System, Just AGI With Three Add-Backs

ACA MAGI is one of those terms that sounds like it requires a decoder ring. The reality is almost boring, and that's good news.

For ACA purposes, modified adjusted gross income generally equals:

> *AGI* plus *tax-exempt interest* plus *non-taxable Social Security benefits* plus *certain excluded foreign income.*

That's it. No mysterious worksheet of lifestyle spending. No hidden formula based on your zip code. It's a tax-return number with three common add-backs.

Those add-backs explain some of the "wait, that counts?" moments:

- *Tax-exempt interest*: Municipal bond interest may be exempt from federal income tax, but it's not invisible for ACA MAGI. It gets added back. The policy logic is simple: tax-exempt doesn't mean you didn't get the money.
- *Non-taxable Social Security*: Social Security benefits can be partly taxable or not taxable depending on other income. Even if a portion is non-taxable, that non-taxable portion is added back for ACA MAGI. Again: the money arrived; the ACA system counts it.
- *Excluded foreign income*: If you have foreign earned income that is excluded from income tax under specific rules, it still tends to be included for ACA MAGI via this add-back concept.

Notice what's *not* on this list: home equity, unrealized gains, credit card rewards, gifts, inheritances, and most of the things that make budgeting messy. ACA MAGI is narrower than real life.

The "Household Income" Number: One More Layer

ACA assistance is based on household income, which is built from ACA MAGI. This is where the earlier "dependents who must file" rule matters.

Household income generally equals the sum of ACA MAGI for each person in the tax household who is counted for this purpose: you, your spouse on a joint return, and any dependents who are required to file. The reason for the "required to file" filter is practical. The IRS doesn't want to pull in a dependent's income that never hits a return.

For planning, household income is the number you're trying to steer. Not because steering is fun, but because the assistance formula can move quickly with income, and the reconciliation process at filing time has sharp edges.

A Concrete Household Example (Without Drowning in Numbers)

Picture a household of three:

- You retire at 60.
- Your spouse is 58 and does some part-time consulting.
- Your 22-year-old child lives at home, works part-time, and you plan to claim them as a dependent.

The tax household size is three. But household income for ACA purposes is not automatically the sum of all three people's wages. It depends on whether the dependent is required to file.

If the dependent's income stays low enough that they aren't required to file, the assistance calculation might effectively be based on just you and your spouse. Household size of three, income from two people. That combination can produce a surprisingly good result.

If the dependent lands a well-paid internship and now must file, their income can join the household income number. Same household size, higher household income. That single change can shrink assistance dramatically, even though nothing changed about your own retirement plan.

This is why planning conversations about dependents shouldn't stop at "Can we claim them?" The better question is "Are we pulling their income into our subsidy math this year?" You can't always control the answer, but you can anticipate it.

The Three Documents That Quietly Run the Show

The paperwork ecosystem is less scary when you know the cast of characters.

Form 1095-A is the statement that reports your health plan premiums and any advance payments of the credit that reduced your monthly bill. It's the receipt the Marketplace hands the IRS (and you) for what happened during the year.

Form 8962 is the reconciliation form filed with your return. It compares:

- what was paid in advance on your behalf, and
- what you were actually eligible for based on final household income.

Publication 974 is the long-form guide the IRS provides for the credit and its edge cases. Most people never need to read it cover to cover. Its value is reassurance: the rules are written down, and strange situations are usually anticipated somewhere.

If you take only one habit from this: keep your 1095-A with the same seriousness as a W-2. If it's missing or wrong, filing cleanly becomes harder, and the reconciliation process can turn into a long, annoying correspondence instead of a simple calculation.

Why Planning Around "Taxable Income" Misses the Target

Many retirees are trained to optimize taxable income: use deductions, manage brackets, harvest losses, keep taxes low. That instinct is excellent—but it's not always the same game as subsidy planning.

Taxable income is calculated *after* subtracting either the standard deduction or itemized deductions. Those deductions can be huge for tax bills, but they generally do *nothing* to reduce AGI. And because ACA MAGI starts at AGI, many beloved tax moves don't move the number that drives health-plan assistance.

That's why someone can say, truthfully, "Our taxable income was almost zero," and still have a high ACA MAGI. A big standard deduction can erase taxable income while leaving AGI standing tall. The subsidy system is looking at the taller number.

If you want the shortest translation:

> *For ACA purposes, above—the-line matters more than below—the-line.*

"Above—the-line" means items that affect AGI directly (income and adjustments). "Below—the-line" means items that affect taxable income after AGI is already set. The below—the-line world still matters for your tax bill. It just isn't the lever arm for assistance.

The Emotional Trap: "But That Money Isn't Really Income"

Early retirement creates money flows that don't match the emotional meaning of income.

Selling shares in a brokerage account might feel like moving money from one pocket to another. But if those shares have gains, part of that sale is income in the IRS narrative and will increase AGI.

A Roth conversion can feel like shuffling accounts. But it's treated as income because you're moving pre-tax money into a tax-free environment. The IRS collects its toll at the moment of conversion, and the subsidy calculation sees the same income spike.

Even municipal bond interest can trigger the "come on" reaction: you bought the bonds precisely because the interest was tax-exempt, and yet it shows up in the ACA MAGI add-back. It's not "taxable," but it's still counted.

These moments aren't moral judgments; they're reminders. The ACA system uses the tax return as a universal measuring stick because it's already audited, standardized, and enforceable. The cost is that it sometimes counts money in a way that doesn't match your internal categories.

A Simple Planning Checklist That Actually Holds Up

Without turning your kitchen table into a CPA office, a few checks keep you from planning around the wrong number:

- *Confirm your filing status for the year* (especially if marriage, divorce, or separation is involved).
- *List who will be claimed as dependents*, and note whether any dependent might be required to file a return.
- *Find last year's AGI* on Form 1040 to anchor expectations.
- *Identify add-backs that turn AGI into ACA MAGI*: tax-exempt interest, non-taxable Social Security, excluded foreign income.
- *Treat big one-time events as household-income events*, not just tax events: asset sales with gains, large IRA distributions, Roth conversions.

None of this requires predicting the future perfectly. It's more like putting bumpers on the bowling lane. You're trying to avoid the specific gutter balls that create ugly surprises at reconciliation time.

Why This Slice of Tax Knowledge Pays Off

Health-plan assistance is generous when you qualify and unforgiving when you misjudge. The system doesn't ask whether you *meant* to overshoot your income estimate. It just compares the advance payments to the final calculation and settles the difference.

Knowing your tax household and the AGI-to-ACA-MAGI bridge gives you something rare in personal finance: a controllable target. Even when spending needs are steady, the income number can swing based on where the money comes from and how events land on the return. That's not a problem to fear. It's a problem you can plan around—once you're aiming at the right bullseye.

3.2 Which Income Sources Count and Why Cash Flow Is Not the Same as MAGI

A checking account is a terrible accountant. It records money arriving and money leaving, but it can't tell you whether a deposit was a paycheck, a gift, a loan, a return of your own principal, or a taxable gain. For ACA planning, that distinction is the whole ballgame. Two households can spend the same $70,000 and have wildly different ACA MAGI, simply because one household's "income" is mostly withdrawals that the IRS counts and the other household's "income" is mostly money that never appears in the ACA MAGI calculation.

A useful habit is to stop calling everything "income" in casual conversation. Start labeling cash sources with two tags:

- *Cash-flow effect*: Does this put spendable dollars in my hands?
- *MAGI effect*: Does this increase the income number that drives ACA affordability?

Sometimes the answer is "yes" to both. Sometimes it's "yes" to only one. And sometimes the answer is "no" to both, in which case you probably misread what happened.

A quick anchor: the ACA MAGI lens is narrower than your life

As already established, ACA MAGI starts with AGI and then adds back a short list of items (notably tax-exempt interest and nontaxable Social Security benefits). That definition matters here because most cash sources enter the system through AGI—or don't. The easiest way to think about the rest of this section is: *Does this cash source show up in AGI? If not, is it one of the add-backs?*

Once you start asking that question, a lot of "I don't get why our assistance dropped" stories become completely predictable.

Wages and salaries: brutally simple, relentlessly counted

If you or your spouse takes a job—full-time, part-time, seasonal, consulting with a W-2 at the end—wages are the cleanest example of cash flow matching MAGI. They land in AGI. They count.

The interesting part isn't the mechanics; it's the way wages tend to arrive. Wages are often "smooth" (a steady stream) while your other retirement cash sources can be lumpy. That smoothness can quietly crowd out room for other moves you might want to make during the year: realizing capital gains, doing a Roth conversion, taking a distribution. Even a modest job can turn a year that would have been a flexible planning playground into a year where every extra dollar has consequences.

One more wrinkle: wage withholding can make a year *feel* like it has less income because the paychecks are smaller. ACA MAGI does not care about withholding. It cares about the gross amount that goes on the return.

Self-employment income: the income source with knobs

Self-employment profit (or loss) is also counted in AGI, but unlike wages, it comes with knobs you can actually turn. Revenue minus ordinary business expenses determines the profit that flows into your income. That doesn't mean you should go hunting for sketchy write-offs; it means timing and legitimate expenses matter more here than almost anywhere else.

Self-employment income also tends to arrive with emotional whiplash: a great month, a dead month, an invoice paid in January instead of December. That volatility is exactly why you want to track year-to-date income during the year rather than guessing.

If you're doing consulting or freelance work in the years before 65, this category deserves special attention because it's both common and surprisingly adjustable in timing. The checking account will show deposits. ACA MAGI will reflect *profit*, not deposits, and not necessarily in the same month.

Pensions and annuities: steady cash, steady MAGI

Pensions are the mirror image of wages: reliable cash flow, reliably counted. Most pension income shows up in AGI and therefore increases ACA MAGI.

Annuities can be trickier. Some annuity payments are partly a return of your principal and partly taxable earnings. The checking account sees a single deposit; the tax system splits it into "counts" and "doesn't count." The more your payment is treated as taxable income, the more it will raise AGI and ACA MAGI.

The planning implication is simple even when the tax details are not: if a pension or annuity is your main spending engine, you may have less room to maneuver on ACA MAGI. That doesn't make it bad income. It just makes it income that uses up your MAGI "budget" quickly.

Social Security: counted even when it's not taxable

Social Security is where people first discover that ACA MAGI has its own personality. On a federal return, Social Security benefits can be partly taxable or even not taxable at all depending on other income. Many people correctly learn the tax rule and then assume, "Great, our Social Security isn't taxable, so it doesn't hurt our assistance."

Then ACA MAGI adds back the non-taxable portion.

So Social Security can reduce assistance even in years where it barely increases taxable income. That can feel like a gotcha, but it's exactly how ACA MAGI is defined: ACA MAGI includes non-taxable Social Security benefits.

In practical terms, Social Security creates a floor under your ACA MAGI. Once benefits start, your baseline income number often rises permanently. That doesn't mean you shouldn't claim Social Security; it means you should anticipate that it takes up space in the income range you're trying to manage.

Interest: ordinary, predictable, and sometimes sneakily added back

Bank interest and taxable bond interest are usually ordinary income. They increase AGI, which increases ACA MAGI. Nothing dramatic there.

The drama comes from *tax-exempt* interest, such as municipal bond interest. Many investors buy municipal bonds precisely because the interest is exempt from federal income tax. That strategy can still be perfectly sensible—but for ACA planning, tax-exempt interest is not invisible. It is added back when computing ACA MAGI.

This is a classic "cash flow vs. MAGI" split:

- Your checking account sees interest deposits.
- Your federal taxable income may not include that interest.
- ACA MAGI includes it anyway, which can reduce assistance.

If you hold municipal bonds in a taxable account and you're counting on significant ACA assistance, treat that interest like a slow leak in your MAGI budget. It may not be huge, but it's persistent and easy to overlook.

Dividends: cash you didn't ask for (and MAGI you can't un-ring)

Dividends are the houseplant of taxable investing: they quietly keep happening even if you ignore them. If you own dividend-paying funds or stocks in a taxable account, you can get taxable dividends whether or not you "need the income," whether or not you reinvest them, and whether or not you touched the account all year.

Reinvested dividends are the perfect example of why the checking account is not the scorekeeper. If dividends are automatically reinvested, you may never see a deposit. Yet those dividends generally still increase AGI and therefore ACA MAGI.

This can surprise people who build a retirement spending plan around "only selling what we need." Dividends can generate taxable income even in a year where you sell nothing. If your investment strategy leans heavily toward dividend funds, recognize that you may be buying yourself a steadier stream of MAGI than you intended.

Capital gains: the voluntary tax event that stops feeling voluntary

Capital gains tend to be the centerpiece of ACA income management because they are partly controllable. A gain becomes real (and usually shows up in AGI) when you sell an appreciated asset in a taxable account. Until you sell, the gain is unrealized and generally not part of MAGI. The day you sell, it becomes realized and joins your income story.

That gives you leverage, but it also gives you responsibility. A household that funds spending by selling appreciated shares is essentially choosing how much MAGI to create each year. That can be empowering: you can sell less in a year where you need to keep ACA MAGI down, and sell more in a year where you have room.

Two caution flags matter:

- *The gain is not the sale proceeds.* Selling $50,000 of stock does not automatically create $50,000 of income. Only the gain portion counts. If your basis is high, your MAGI impact may be modest. If your basis is low, the same sale can spike MAGI.
- *Rebalancing can create gains even if spending is unchanged.* People often rebalance to reduce risk, shift into bonds, or simplify holdings. That's a portfolio decision, but in a taxable account it can also be an income decision.

Capital gains can be taxed at favorable long-term rates, which is wonderful for your federal tax bill. ACA MAGI does not care that the rate is favorable. A dollar of long-term capital gain still increases AGI, which increases ACA MAGI.

Traditional IRA and 401(k) withdrawals: cash with a MAGI price tag

Withdrawals from traditional tax-deferred accounts (traditional IRA, traditional 401(k), and similar plans) are among the most MAGI-dense ways to fund spending. In general, distributions are taxable and included in gross income, which increases AGI and therefore ACA MAGI.

This is the classic early retirement trap: you built up a large traditional account (because that was smart during working years), and now the account does exactly what it promised to do—it produces taxable income when you take money out. If you take $60,000 out to live on, it can be close to $60,000 of added income for ACA purposes (basis complications aside).

That doesn't make these accounts "bad." It means they are powerful and blunt instruments. If you need to keep ACA MAGI within a specific range to keep coverage affordable, large traditional distributions can blow past that range fast.

Roth IRA withdrawals: spendable dollars that often barely register

Qualified Roth IRA distributions are the closest thing to "clean" spending money in the ACA world. If a Roth withdrawal is qualified, it is not included in gross income. If it's not in gross income, it generally doesn't increase AGI, and therefore it generally doesn't increase ACA MAGI.

Even better, the return of regular Roth contributions (your original contributions) is typically not included in gross income either. That means Roth assets can provide real spending power without pushing up the income number used for ACA affordability.

Two important cautions keep this from turning into a fairy tale:

- Roth withdrawals can be qualified or not depending on rules and timing. Non-qualified distributions can have taxable portions.
- Pulling from Roth accounts is still a strategic decision; using them too aggressively can leave you with fewer tools later.

Still, the core cash-flow-versus-MAGI split is striking: Roth dollars can pay for groceries without showing up as income on the ACA scoreboard.

Roth conversions: no cash, lots of MAGI

Roth conversions are the mirror opposite of Roth withdrawals. A conversion from a traditional IRA to a Roth IRA generally increases gross income (and therefore AGI and ACA MAGI), even though you may not receive a single dollar of spendable cash.

This is where many planners get whiplash. They see a conversion as "moving money from one pocket to another," and operationally, that's true. But the tax system treats it as realizing previously untaxed income. ACA MAGI follows the tax system.

So conversions are a MAGI event without a cash-flow benefit. That doesn't mean conversions are bad; it means conversions are not "free," and the cost isn't only the income tax bill. The cost can also be reduced ACA assistance for the year of the conversion.

If you ever want proof that cash flow and MAGI are different concepts, Roth conversions are Exhibit A.

Taxable account withdrawals: three different things hiding in one transaction

A withdrawal from a taxable brokerage account can be any combination of:

- return of your original principal (not income),
- realized capital gain (income), and
- dividends and interest generated along the way (often income whether or not you withdrew anything).

The checking account sees a transfer. The IRS sees a mix of categories, only some of which affect AGI.

This is why one retiree can "withdraw" $70,000 from a brokerage account and show only $15,000 of capital gains, while another withdraws $70,000 and shows $50,000 of gains. Same lifestyle. Different basis. Different investment history. Different ACA MAGI.

If you're trying to forecast MAGI, you can't just assume "we'll spend $X from taxable." You need at least a rough sense of the gain percentage in what you plan to sell.

Cash savings and CDs: principal is not income, but interest is

Spending down a bank savings account is mostly moving your own money back into your hands. The principal you withdraw doesn't increase AGI and doesn't increase ACA MAGI. But the interest the account throws off does.

This makes cash savings unusually ACA-friendly as a spending bridge. It's not tax-free magic; it's simply that using saved principal is not the same as generating income. The trade-off is opportunity cost: money sitting in cash may grow more slowly than money invested. Whether that's worth it depends on your broader plan, but from a pure ACA lens, cash reserves can function like a pressure-release valve.

CDs behave similarly: spending the principal doesn't count; the interest does.

HSA reimbursements: stealth spending power (with paperwork discipline)

Health Savings Account (HSA) reimbursements are another example of spendable dollars that can avoid showing up in AGI when done correctly. If you pay qualified medical expenses out of pocket and later reimburse yourself from the HSA, that reimbursement is generally not taxable. No gross income, no AGI increase, no ACA MAGI increase.

The catch is documentation. An HSA isn't a casual "health slush fund." The power comes from the rules, and the rules come with receipts. If you keep good records, HSAs can provide a pool of tax-free, MAGI-light cash for healthcare costs in particular.

Gifts, inheritances, and loans: real cash, usually not MAGI

These show up often in real households and almost never in neat retirement calculators.

A gift from a family member can increase your cash flow without increasing AGI. An inheritance can deliver a large pile of spendable assets without showing up as ordinary income on your return (though income generated by inherited assets can count later). A loan proceeds deposit is not income.

The planning caution is behavioral, not technical: "It hit the account, so it must be income" is wrong often enough to be dangerous. If you receive a one-time gift or inheritance, don't assume it will wreck ACA affordability. It might not. The effect depends on what you do next (sell assets with gains, earn interest, receive dividends), not on the mere arrival of money.

Two households, $70,000 spending, very different ACA MAGI

Consider two retirees with the same lifestyle: $70,000 of annual spending. No wages. Same age. Same zip code. Same plan options. Their budgets look identical.

Household A funds $70,000 mostly from qualified Roth IRA distributions and cash savings. They also have a small amount of interest and dividends. Their ACA MAGI might be relatively low because the largest cash sources are not included in gross income.

Household B funds $70,000 mostly from traditional IRA distributions and selling appreciated shares in a taxable account. They also have dividends. Their ACA MAGI can be substantially higher because those cash sources largely increase AGI.

Nothing about Household B is irresponsible. They're simply using accounts that were designed to be taxed upon withdrawal. But from an ACA affordability standpoint, Household A has a quieter income profile even though both households live the same life.

That's the heart of the cash-flow-versus-MAGI lesson: the assistance system does not subsidize "need" as measured by spending. It subsidizes based on an income definition, and your choice of cash source can move that number more than your lifestyle does.

A practical way to label your own cash sources

If you want a simple, sticky way to organize your plan, sort each cash source into one of these buckets:

- *MAGI-heavy*: wages, self-employment profit, pensions, taxable interest, most traditional retirement distributions, realized capital gains.
- *MAGI-light*: taxable brokerage withdrawals with high basis (small gains), partial-taxable annuity payments, strategies that create some income but not dollar-for-dollar.

- *Mostly MAGI-neutral*: spending down cash principal, qualified Roth IRA distributions, return of Roth contributions, HSA reimbursements for qualified expenses, loans, gifts (with caveats).

The goal isn't to eliminate MAGI-heavy sources. The goal is to recognize them early enough that you can choose *when* and *how much* to use them, instead of discovering in March that your "simple withdrawal" was also an income spike.

The most common confusion points (and the quick fixes)

A few misunderstandings show up over and over because they're so reasonable from a human perspective.

"Reinvested dividends don't count because we didn't take the cash." Reinvesting is still receiving; you just immediately used the cash to buy more shares. The income usually still counts.

"Long-term capital gains don't matter much because the tax rate is low." The tax rate may be low; the income still increases AGI and therefore ACA MAGI.

"Municipal bond interest is tax-free, so it's safe." It may be exempt from federal income tax, but it is added back for ACA MAGI.

"A Roth conversion didn't put money in our pocket, so it shouldn't count." Conversions generally increase gross income, raising AGI and ACA MAGI without providing spendable cash.

Once those points click, ACA planning starts to feel less like guesswork and more like choosing which levers to pull. The checking account is still useful for paying bills. It's just not the instrument panel for ACA affordability. The instrument panel is the income definition, and the steering wheel is the set of choices you make about where your spending money comes from.

3.3 Deductions, Adjustments, and Other Legitimate MAGI Levers

There's a particular kind of frustration that hits in mid-March: you did "all the tax-smart things," your taxable income looks impressively low, and yet your ACA affordability math didn't improve much at all. That's not bad luck. It's usually a category error. Plenty of popular deductions reduce *taxable income* without touching the number that drives ACA savings.

The trick is to stop thinking in terms of "deductions" as one big bucket. The IRS doesn't. The return has a fault line running straight through it: items that change *adjusted gross income* (AGI) live above the line, and items that reduce taxable income live below it. Since ACA MAGI is built from AGI (plus a few add-backs), the levers that matter most are the ones that reduce AGI in the first place.

If you remember nothing else, remember this: a move can be wonderful for your tax bill and *irrelevant* for your ACA number. That's not unfair; it's just the structure.

The MAGI levers that actually move the needle

It helps to think of MAGI management like weight control with a picky scale. Your scale doesn't care that you switched to a smaller plate (itemized deductions). It cares about what actually changed your body (AGI). The practical MAGI levers are the adjustments that reduce AGI—the "above—the-line" reductions that show up before the standard deduction or itemized deductions are even considered.

AGI, in IRS terms, is gross income minus specific adjustments (often those on Schedule 1). That's where the real ACA levers tend to sit. Itemized deductions, charitable giving, and the standard deduction matter for federal tax owed, but they generally do not reduce AGI, and therefore generally do not reduce ACA MAGI.

This distinction is liberating. It means you can stop chasing every shiny deduction and focus on the handful of moves that have a double payoff: they reduce taxes *and* they can preserve ACA affordability.

Three buckets: a better way to sort "tax moves"

Before getting specific, it's worth sorting common planning ideas into three buckets. This prevents the most common misunderstanding: assuming any tax break is a MAGI lever.

- *Bucket A: Changes AGI* (often a real ACA lever). These are adjustments and business-profit reducers that flow into AGI.
- *Bucket B: Changes only taxable income* (good for taxes, usually not for ACA). Standard deduction and most itemized deductions live here.
- *Bucket C: Changes cash flow only* (budget help, usually not an ACA lever). Think of using cash principal, borrowing, gifts, reimbursements—helpful, but not a line on the return.

The goal is not to cram your life into buckets; it's to avoid the expensive mistake of celebrating a Bucket B win while expecting a Bucket A outcome.

HSA contributions: the rare "clean" lever (when you're eligible)

If you are eligible to contribute to an HSA, you've found one of the most satisfying levers available: a contribution can reduce AGI, which can reduce ACA MAGI, and the account itself can later fund qualified medical expenses tax-free. It's like getting paid twice for being organized.

Eligibility is the gatekeeper. You generally need to be covered by an HSA-qualified high-deductible health plan (HDHP) and meet other IRS requirements. If you have that kind of plan, HSA contributions become unusually powerful during the pre-65 years because medical spending is often rising just as you're trying to keep income in a specific range.

Two nuances make HSAs especially relevant for ACA planning:

- *Timing flexibility*: Depending on your circumstances, you may be able to make contributions during the year and sometimes up until the tax filing deadline for that tax year. That can make an HSA contribution a true "year-end lever" when you discover your income is running hot.
- *It's an adjustment, not an itemized deduction*: That means it can reduce AGI rather than merely reducing taxable income after AGI is already set. For ACA purposes, that's the key feature.

HSAs also have a personality trait that matters for household planning: they reward discipline. An HSA contribution that reduces AGI is clean on paper, but only if you're actually eligible and you track it correctly. The IRS is not sentimental about accidental contributions.

Self-employed health insurance deduction: a lever that can interact with ACA math

For people with self-employment income, one of the most meaningful above—the-line deductions can be health insurance premiums. This can be both powerful and tricky in the years you're buying insurance through the exchange. Publication 974 exists largely because the interactions can get complicated, including circular calculations in some cases.

The practical takeaway is still useful even without swimming into the deep end: if you have self-employment income, there may be legitimate ways to treat health insurance premiums in a way that reduces AGI. That can help your ACA number *and* reduce taxes, but the mechanics can be sensitive to your exact situation and the way credits are computed.

If you're self-employed and doing ACA planning, this is one of the places where DIY planning should come with humility. It's not that you can't understand it; it's that tiny differences in facts can change the right answer. The clean move is to flag it early and, if needed, use Publication 974 (or a competent preparer) as the referee.

Retirement plan contributions (for workers who are "sort of" retired)

A surprising number of people in the pre-65 window aren't fully retired in the Hollywood sense. They're "retired" but doing contract work, working part-time, or running a small business that they enjoy. If you have earned income, retirement plan contributions may still be available and may reduce AGI, depending on the plan type and your circumstances.

From an ACA lens, these contributions can be appealing because they convert earned income—the most MAGI-dense kind of cash—into sheltered retirement savings while also lowering the income number used for ACA affordability.

The tension is obvious: contributing to retirement accounts reduces today's spendable cash. That trade-off is more palatable in years where you have other cash sources (taxable savings, Roth principal, cash reserves) and want to keep ACA MAGI from drifting upward.

The key planning posture: if you're earning income, don't ignore retirement contributions just because you're "already retired." In the ACA years, a contribution can be less about building a bigger nest egg and more about buying flexibility in the affordability formula.

IRA deductions: sometimes available, sometimes not

Traditional IRA contributions can sometimes be deductible, and when they are, they can reduce AGI. That makes them potentially useful for ACA MAGI management. The catch is that deductibility depends on your income and whether you (or a spouse) are covered by an employer retirement plan, among other factors. In the pre-65 window, those variables can change from year to year.

If you're in a year where the deduction is available, it can behave like a clean lever: you move money into a tax-deferred account and reduce AGI at the same time. But this is not a lever to assume. It's a lever to verify.

A small but important mindset shift helps here: the best MAGI levers are boring. They're not loopholes. They're the predictable result of rules that were written to encourage certain behaviors (saving for retirement, saving for healthcare). The only drama comes from eligibility and phaseouts, not from trickery.

Student loan interest and other smaller adjustments: useful, but don't overbuild around them

Some above—the-line adjustments are real but modest. Student loan interest is a common example for households that still have loans in these years (either their own or through family arrangements). Certain educator expenses, moving expenses for military members, and similar items can exist in the ecosystem.

From an ACA perspective, these can be worth capturing if you're near an income threshold and the adjustment is available. But they are rarely the centerpiece of a plan because they're not always controllable and often not large.

Treat them like weatherstripping. Helpful, incremental, and not a substitute for insulation.

The standard deduction: a tax gift that does not lower ACA MAGI

The standard deduction is one of the most misunderstood pieces of ACA planning because it's so central to how people think about "income." It can dramatically reduce taxable income. It can even reduce your federal tax bill to zero. And it generally does *nothing* to reduce AGI.

So if you're hoping that "keeping taxable income low" will automatically preserve ACA affordability, the standard deduction can set a trap. You can have:

- a low tax bill, and
- a high ACA MAGI.

That combination is not rare. It's practically a signature move for households living on traditional IRA withdrawals and long-term gains: taxable income looks modest thanks to deductions, but AGI remains substantial.

This is why the phrase "our taxable income will be about $X" is not a reliable planning statement for ACA affordability. The more useful phrase is "our AGI will be about $X," because that's what feeds ACA MAGI.

Itemized deductions: great for taxes, usually not the ACA lever you want

Itemizing can be valuable. Mortgage interest, state and local taxes (within limits), charitable gifts, and medical expenses can change your tax bill. But itemized deductions generally do not change AGI. They arrive after AGI is already set.

So itemizing often lands in Bucket B: it changes taxable income, not AGI. It can still matter indirectly, because a lower tax bill may make it easier to choose cash sources that are more MAGI-friendly. But that's a second-order effect. The itemized deduction itself is usually not the direct lever.

Charitable giving is a perfect example. Many households give more in retirement, not less. Giving is meaningful, but from an ACA perspective it's easy to overestimate the income impact. Unless the giving changes AGI (which generally it does not), the ACA number may not move.

Business expenses: the legitimate way to shrink self-employment profit

For those with self-employment income, reducing profit through legitimate business expenses can reduce AGI. This is one of the few areas where the phrase "expense it" is both common and often misunderstood.

The useful version of the idea is not "buy stuff to dodge taxes." It's "be intentional about timing and classification of expenses you would incur anyway." If you need a laptop, software, liability insurance, professional dues, continuing education, or a home office that meets the rules, those items can reduce net profit. Reduced net profit reduces income on the return. That reduces AGI. That can reduce ACA MAGI.

The warning label: self-employment categories are audited more often than daydreams. If an expense isn't ordinary and necessary for your business, don't try to force it. The goal is sustainable, defensible planning, not a risky one-year stunt.

Tax-loss harvesting: not the lever many think it is

Selling investments at a loss (tax-loss harvesting) can be useful in managing taxes, and it can offset capital gains. But it's not a universal "reduce my MAGI" tool in the way people sometimes imagine.

A realized loss can reduce your net capital gains, which can reduce AGI. That can help. But the effect depends on what gains you have and how the loss is used. In some years, harvesting a loss simply creates a carryforward to future years. That may still be valuable, but it may not solve the current-year ACA problem you're trying to solve.

The better posture is to treat tax-loss harvesting as a strategic tool for smoothing investment taxation, not as a reliable emergency brake for ACA MAGI. Sometimes it helps beautifully. Sometimes it's a gentle tap.

A subtle lever: choosing deductions that change AGI vs. deductions that merely change your bill

One of the most practical ways to avoid frustration is to ask a blunt question about any "tax move" you're considering:

> Does this change AGI, or does it only change taxable income?

If it changes AGI, it's potentially a direct ACA lever. If it only changes taxable income, treat it as a tax-bill optimization—still worth doing, but don't expect it to rescue your affordability calculation.

This question also helps you communicate with a tax preparer. Instead of a vague "we need our income lower," you can say, "We're trying to manage AGI because it drives ACA MAGI. Are there any above—the-line adjustments we're missing?" That one sentence tends to change the quality of the conversation.

A year-end MAGI lever checklist (the kind you can actually use)

The best levers tend to be the ones you can still pull in November or December, when you have enough information to know whether your income is running above or below your target range. Here's a practical checklist to run before the year closes:

- *HSA contribution (if eligible)*: Increase contributions if you have room and cash to do it.
- *Self-employment profit review*: Check year-to-date profit, confirm business expenses are properly captured, and consider timing for legitimate expenses or invoicing.
- *Retirement contributions tied to earned income*: If you have wages or self-employment income, confirm whether additional contributions are available and beneficial.
- *Self-employed health insurance deduction implications*: If self-employed, flag this for careful handling given its interaction

with ACA credits; consider consulting Publication 974 or a knowledgeable preparer.

- *Don't overcount the standard deduction*: Enjoy it for tax savings, but don't mistake it for an ACA lever.

Notice what's missing: elaborate schemes, exotic shelters, frantic December trades. The strongest MAGI management is usually boring, legal, and repeatable.

The point of levers isn't to "game" the system

A good plan doesn't treat ACA affordability as a loophole contest. It treats it as coordination. The affordability formula is an income test based on AGI-derived definitions, so you coordinate your cash sources and deductions with that reality.

That mindset also protects you from a common mistake: pushing too hard on one lever because it "works," then creating a different problem later. For example, maxing every possible deduction might lower AGI today but leave you short on cash, forcing a larger traditional IRA withdrawal that erases the benefit. The most useful levers are the ones that fit naturally into how you live and how you want to fund your spending.

Publication 974 exists because these interactions are real. You don't need to memorize it. You just need to respect that the system has moving parts—and that the cleanest way to influence ACA MAGI is usually to focus on what changes AGI.

Once you start sorting actions by whether they affect AGI, the noise drops away. The standard deduction becomes what it is: a tax break, not an affordability tool. Itemizing becomes a tax choice, not a subsidy strategy. And the levers that remain—HSA contributions, self-employment profit management, certain above—the-line adjustments—stand out clearly enough to use on purpose rather than by accident.

3.4 Timing Income, Gains, and Distributions Across Tax Years

The calendar is an underrated financial weapon. Not because January is magical, but because the ACA affordability math keeps score by tax year. The year closes, the books close, and whatever landed between January 1 and December 31 becomes your official income story—even if the transactions were separated by a weekend and a couple of clicks.

That's why timing is more than "tax planning." It's also health-insurance planning. A single decision to sell shares on December 31 instead of January 2 can move a taxable event across a boundary that the subsidy system treats as a concrete wall. Same investment. Same life. Different year. Different outcome.

The most helpful mindset is to stop treating income as a thing that "happens to you" and start treating it as something you *schedule*. Some income is uncontrollable (a required payout, an unexpected severance, a mutual fund distribution you didn't ask for). But a surprising amount of what drives ACA MAGI in the pre-65 window comes from choices that can be delayed, accelerated, or spread out.

Why timing matters so much: the annual scorecard and the reconciliation bill

Advance payments of the premium tax credit are paid during the year based on an estimate. The final credit is determined later based on actual income for that tax year. When your estimate and reality diverge, the system reconciles the difference at filing time. The reconciliation itself isn't the problem; surprises are.

Late-year surprises sting more than early-year ones because they arrive when there's no time left to respond. If you discover in February that your income estimate was low, you can adjust course. If you discover on December 29 that you're about to realize a big gain or take a large distribution, you're often stuck with it. That's how "we'll deal with it later" turns into a repayment check.

The calendar, then, is a control surface. It won't make income non-taxable. But it can often decide *which year* gets the income—and that can decide whether you stayed in your intended ACA range or over-shot it.

Taxable events that are often schedule-able

Not every dollar is movable. Wages arrive when they arrive. A pension pays on its schedule. Social Security has its own rhythm. Still, the usual suspects in ACA MAGI management are often the ones you can manipulate:

- Realizing gains by selling appreciated assets in a taxable account (reported through the Schedule D / Form 8949 framework and flowing into Form 1040).
- Taking distributions from traditional retirement accounts.
- Executing Roth conversions (income without spendable cash).
- Choosing whether to do one large transaction or several smaller ones across time.

In other words: the transactions you initiate are the transactions you can calendar. That's a comforting thought, because those are often the same transactions that cause the biggest swings in ACA affordability.

Bunching vs. spreading: the simplest timing choice

The most common timing mistake is not "selling at the wrong time." It's *bunching* taxable activity into a single year because it's psychologically tidy.

People love tidy. "Let's just do the whole conversion this year." "Let's simplify the portfolio now." "Let's sell the entire position and be done with it." Tidiness has benefits: fewer accounts, fewer decisions, fewer loose ends.

But tidiness can be expensive if it turns a manageable two-year plan into a one-year income spike. The subsidy system doesn't grade on a multi-year average. It grades each year separately. So "doing it all at once" can take a year that would have qualified for meaningful assistance and turn it into a year of full-price premiums—followed by a calm year where you wish you had more income room.

This is where spreading becomes powerful. Spreading doesn't require fancy optimization. It's often as simple as turning one big taxable event into two medium ones on opposite sides of December 31.

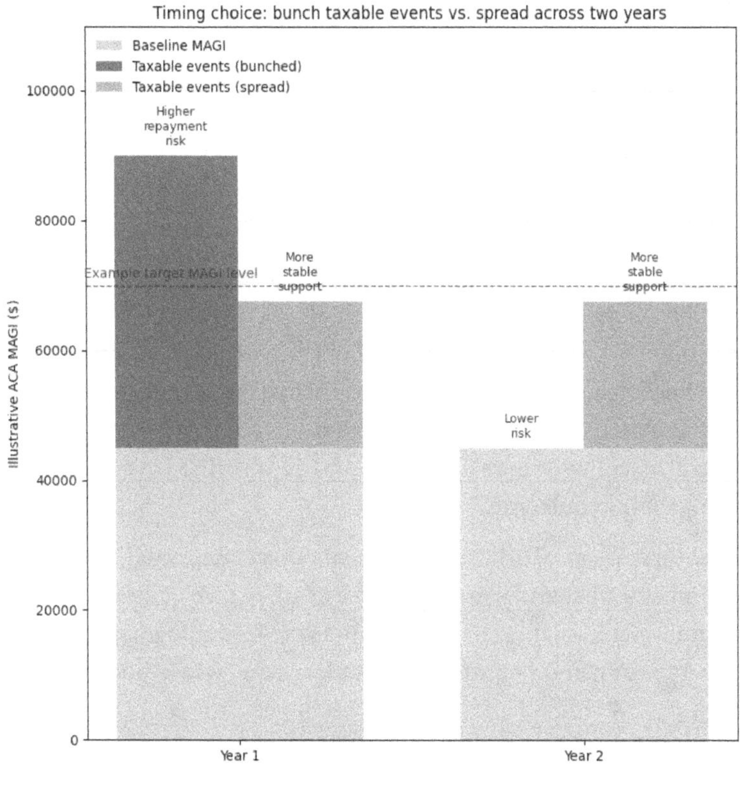

The point isn't that spreading always wins. The point is that spreading often gives you *options*. A bunched year can become so income-heavy that you lose flexibility: no room for additional gains, no room for conversion, no room for surprise dividends, no room for a spouse's small consulting project. A spread plan is usually more forgiving.

The December/January lever: the two-day choice with four-figure consequences

The cleanest timing lever is the boundary between years. If you control the date of a sale or distribution, you often control which tax year gets the income. That's true even if the cash moves almost immediately either way.

Consider a simple example: you intend to realize $20,000 of long-term gains to fund a renovation. You can place the trade on December 31 or on January 2. Your bank account ends up in the same place by the end of January. But your ACA MAGI for the year that just ended is either $20,000 higher or not.

This is not about "timing the market." It's about timing *recognition*. Capital gains are reported through the Schedule D / Form 8949 pipeline and flow into Form 1040 once realized. The moment the gain becomes realized, it belongs to that year's income story. If that year is already crowded, moving the sale a few days forward can protect your assistance eligibility and reduce the odds of a nasty reconciliation outcome.

Of course, it can work in the opposite direction too. If you have a low-income year and you want to use it—to realize gains at favorable tax rates, to rebalance, to simplify holdings—pulling gains into the current year can be smart. The calendar lever swings both ways.

Spreading isn't only about two years—it's also about multiple transactions

People naturally treat a financial decision as a single event: "We're selling the fund." "We're withdrawing from the IRA." But the IRS treats your year as the sum of all events. That opens a simple technique: split a large move into a series.

Instead of selling $80,000 of shares in one shot, you might sell $10,000 each month and watch your projected MAGI in real time. Instead of converting $100,000 to Roth in December, you might convert $8,000 to $10,000 per month and stop when you've reached the top of your intended range.

That kind of pacing does two things:

- It reduces the risk of overshooting because you're measuring as you go.
- It reduces regret because you can stop without having to "undo" anything.

There's a psychological benefit too: smaller moves create fewer "all-or-nothing" days. Most planning failures aren't caused by arithmetic; they're caused by one decisive day where you were busy, tired, or annoyed and wanted the decision off your plate.

Mutual fund distributions: income that arrives without asking permission

Not all timing is yours to control. Taxable accounts can generate lumpy income that simply shows up, especially through year-end mutual fund distributions. Many funds distribute capital gains near the end of the year. Even if you didn't sell anything, the fund may have, and it can pass those gains through to you.

This is why "we didn't sell any shares" is not the same sentence as "we didn't realize any gains." A fund can hand you taxable income while you're innocently making coffee.

Two practical defenses help:

- Pay attention to capital gain distribution estimates for funds you hold in taxable accounts, especially later in the year.
- Favor tax-efficient holdings in taxable accounts if ACA affordability is a major goal. (You don't need perfection; you just need fewer nasty surprises.)

The main lesson is emotional: surprises are rarely "random." They're often a predictable feature of what you own. If a holding has a history of big year-end distributions, treat that as a recurring appointment, not an act of God.

Traditional account distributions: timing is sometimes controllable, sometimes not

Withdrawals from traditional IRAs and 401(k)s are typically taxable and therefore show up in AGI. Timing can matter because you may be able to choose *when* you withdraw and *how much*.

If you're living on these accounts, the obvious danger is taking a large distribution late in the year because "we'll need it for taxes" or "we've been meaning to refill cash." That can be particularly painful if you've been receiving advance subsidies based on an income estimate that assumed a smaller withdrawal schedule.

A cleaner approach is to set a planned distribution cadence early in the year—monthly or quarterly—and treat it like payroll. Not because routine is morally superior, but because routine prevents last-minute panic. Panic is where people write a $40,000 distribution check to themselves on December 15 and then act surprised that their income story changed.

Some distributions are not optional, depending on age and account type. But many pre-65 households still have discretion. Discretion is valuable; use it on purpose.

Roth conversions: the timing lever with no cash cushion

Roth conversions deserve special respect in timing discussions because they create income without providing spendable dollars. That combination makes them uniquely capable of causing subsidy trouble. You can't "fund the repayment" with the conversion itself because the conversion didn't produce cash.

That doesn't mean conversions are off-limits. It means conversions should rarely be done impulsively at year-end. If conversions are part of your long-term plan, pacing them throughout the year can be far safer. It also gives you an escape hatch: if you receive unexpected income later in the year (a surprise distribution, a part-time job, a larger-than-expected gain), you can simply stop converting.

Conversions are a perfect example of why timing is a practical household skill. The best time to manage a conversion is not April; it's while you still have months left to adjust.

A simple forecasting habit: the quarterly MAGI "temperature check"

You don't need a complicated spreadsheet to avoid year-end surprises. You need a recurring moment where you look at the year and ask, "If nothing changes, where will our AGI land?" Then remember the add-backs that turn it into ACA MAGI.

A surprisingly effective cadence is quarterly:

- After Q1, you're learning the year's rhythm.
- After Q2, you can still make meaningful course corrections.
- After Q3, you should be in "protect the estimate" mode.

- In early December, you want a final projection and a short list of allowable moves.

The goal is not to forecast down to the dollar. The goal is to avoid being wrong by $30,000 because you never looked.

If you use tax software or a preparer, you can still do this. Ask for a projection. Or run a rough version yourself using year-to-date income documents and brokerage statements. The only wrong move is waiting for February to discover what happened.

Using low-income years intentionally (instead of accidentally wasting them)

The calendar isn't only a defensive tool. It can also help you *use* a low-income year.

A low-income year is valuable real estate. It may allow you to realize gains, do modest conversions, rebalance a portfolio, or sell a concentrated position while staying within your intended income range. If you waste that year by doing nothing and then cram the same actions into a higher-income year later, you've traded flexibility for procrastination.

This is especially relevant in years right after leaving work. The first year without a salary often has a built-in dip in income, sometimes dramatically so. That year can be an opportunity to do actions that would be painful later—as long as you recognize the opportunity before December is over.

The "crowded year" rule: protect it, don't decorate it

Some years are crowded no matter how well you plan:

- a severance package,
- a home sale with taxable gain components,
- a big pension start,

- a spouse returning to work,
- a one-time business windfall,
- an inherited IRA distribution.

In a crowded year, the best move is often restraint. Don't stack additional taxable activity on top just because it's convenient. Avoid elective gains. Avoid elective conversions. Avoid unnecessary rebalancing in taxable accounts. A crowded year already has enough going on.

This is not timid planning; it's prioritization. Crowded years are the ones most likely to produce APTC repayment issues because your income estimate becomes stale quickly. Keeping additional discretionary income out of those years is one of the most reliable ways to reduce unpleasant mail from the IRS.

The "uncrowded year" rule: use it, but don't get greedy

The opposite trap is getting greedy in a calm year. You project a low AGI and think, "Great—we'll do the full conversion, sell the whole position, and maybe take an extra distribution too." Then the market moves, dividends are higher than expected, or a fund distribution appears, and suddenly the calm year isn't calm.

A better approach is to treat the gap between your projected MAGI and the top of your intended range as a reserve. Use some of it intentionally, but keep a buffer. Buffers are boring; buffers also keep you out of trouble.

One last timing detail: trade dates and settlement dates

For taxable investing, what matters for recognizing a gain is generally the trade date, not when the cash settles. That means waiting until "the money clears" can be the wrong mental model. If you plan to move a sale into January, placing the trade on December 31 because "it won't settle until next week" may not give you the result you want.

The safest approach is simple: if the year boundary matters, don't cut it close. Give yourself a few business days and remove doubt from the equation.

A practical year-end script (the kind that prevents regret)

A strong December routine is short and slightly paranoid:

- Check year-to-date income sources that are already locked in.
- Estimate any remaining unavoidable income (interest, dividends, scheduled payments).
- Decide whether you have room for elective actions: gains, distributions, conversions.
- If you do, schedule them. If you don't, postpone them.
- If your estimate has changed materially, update it to reduce reconciliation shock.

This isn't about perfection. It's about taking control of the one thing you often *can* control: timing.

The calendar will keep turning whether you pay attention or not. Paying attention is what turns timing from an accident into a tool—and turns subsidy reconciliation from a surprise bill into a predictable calculation.

3.5 Roth Conversions and Withdrawal Sequencing Under ACA Rules

A Roth conversion is a strange kind of financial alchemy: you take money that has never been taxed, move it into a Roth account, and volunteer to pay the tax bill now so the future can be cleaner. Done thoughtfully, it can lower lifetime taxes, reduce future required distributions, and give you a bigger pool of tax-free spending later.

Done carelessly in the pre-65 window, it can also turn a year of reasonably priced coverage into a year of full-price premiums—and then hand you the receipt at reconciliation time.

That tension is the whole story. Conversions are not "good" or "bad." They're powerful. And in the years before Medicare, powerful things need guardrails.

Why conversions collide with ACA affordability

Traditional-to-Roth conversions are generally includible in gross income (subject to basis rules), increasing AGI/MAGI and potentially reducing ACA subsidies. That single sentence explains why conversions feel different now than they did during peak-earning years. It's not only the tax bracket you're watching. It's the income-based affordability system running in parallel.

The conversion amount can also be deceptive because it often arrives without cash. If you convert $50,000 from a traditional IRA to a Roth IRA, your spending ability might not change at all that day—yet your income number for the year jumps. That makes conversions uniquely capable of creating a planning hangover: you didn't spend more, but your costs still rise.

The other half of the collision is policy uncertainty. Because enhanced premium tax credits expired at the end of 2025, conversion decisions may be more likely to trigger a large subsidy change in 2026+ if a subsidy cliff is back in effect. In plain language: the penalty for overshooting your intended income range may be steeper than it was recently, so precision matters more.

Withdrawal sequencing: the real "control panel"

Most households don't run into trouble because they did a single conversion. They run into trouble because they funded spending in a way that left them no room to convert *or* they converted in a way that left them no room to fund spending.

Withdrawal sequencing is simply the plan for where your spending money will come from, year after year. Under ACA rules, the "best" sequence is rarely a fixed rule like "taxable first, then IRA, then Roth." It's more like a mixing board. You adjust the sliders each year based on:

- the income level you want to land on for ACA purposes,
- the tax bracket you're willing to fill,
- the size of your cash reserve,
- your taxable account's embedded gains (high basis vs. low basis),
- and how urgently you want to move money out of traditional accounts before Medicare.

If that sounds like a lot, here's the simplifying insight: you don't need a perfect sequence. You need a *flexible* sequence. Flexibility is what lets you respond to the year you actually get.

The ACA-friendly trio: cash, high-basis taxable sales, and qualified Roth withdrawals

In the pre-65 window, three funding sources tend to provide spending power without forcing your income number upward dollar-for-dollar:

- *Cash and cash equivalents*: spending principal is usually not an income event.
- *Taxable brokerage sales with high basis*: selling shares where most of the sale is principal and only a small portion is gain can be remarkably MAGI-efficient.
- *Qualified Roth IRA distributions (and return of regular Roth contributions)*: qualified Roth IRA distributions (and return of reg-

ular Roth contributions) are not included in gross income, so they can provide spendable cash flow with little/no MAGI impact when rules are satisfied.

These sources are valuable not because they eliminate taxes forever, but because they buy you room. Room for what? Often, room for a conversion amount that you choose deliberately rather than one you're forced into.

A useful way to think about this is that spending and converting are two separate jobs. Spending needs cash. Converting needs income capacity. The trio above helps you get cash without consuming as much income capacity, which can leave space to do conversions intentionally.

The IRA withdrawal: sometimes necessary, often expensive (in ACA terms)

Traditional IRA/401(k) distributions remain a core spending source for many households. There's nothing wrong with that. But from an ACA standpoint, they are "expensive" because they tend to raise AGI and therefore ACA MAGI.

That expense can be worth paying in some years. For example, if you're already above your intended income range due to other events, a traditional withdrawal may not meaningfully worsen the situation. Or if you're choosing between a large taxable gain and a traditional withdrawal, you might prefer the traditional withdrawal for other tax reasons.

The danger is habitual withdrawals that mechanically fill your spending gap even when you have MAGI-lighter options available. In the years before Medicare, habits deserve scrutiny.

Roth conversions as a planned "income fill"

Here's a mental model that helps: treat a Roth conversion as "income fill" up to a chosen ceiling.

You start the year with income you can't easily move (pension, interest, dividends, maybe some work). Then you choose how to fund spending. If you fund spending with MAGI-light sources, you may find yourself with unused "income headroom"—room before you hit the top of your intended ACA range.

A Roth conversion can fill that room on purpose. Not because you enjoy paying tax early, but because a controlled conversion can accomplish long-term goals (reducing future RMDs, building Roth assets, smoothing future brackets) while keeping current-year healthcare affordability in bounds.

This flips the emotional framing. Instead of "Should we do a conversion this year?" the question becomes "How much room do we have for conversion income this year after funding spending?"

That question is usually easier to answer and harder to mess up.

Three illustrative household strategies (same spending, different mixes)

The examples below use round numbers to highlight mechanics, not to suggest a universally "right" outcome. Suppose a household needs $80,000 to live on, and already expects $30,000 of baseline income that will show up in AGI (interest, dividends, maybe a small pension).

	Strategy A: IRA-heavy	*Strategy B: MAGI-light spending + conversion*	*Strategy C: Roth-heavy (conversion minimal)*
Spending source	Mostly traditional IRA distributions	Cash + high-basis taxable sales + some Roth withdrawals	Mostly qualified Roth withdrawals + cash
Typical AGI impact of spending	High (withdrawals largely count)	Moderate (only gains portion counts; Roth qualified withdrawals often don't)	Low (Roth qualified withdrawals often don't)
Conversion room available	Small (income already high)	Meaningful (room exists by design)	Large in theory, but may not be needed
Long-term effect	Traditional accounts remain large; future RMD pressure	Traditional accounts shrink steadily; Roth grows	Roth shrinks; traditional may remain large

What's interesting here is not which strategy is best. It's that Strategy B creates a deliberate *trade*: use MAGI-light sources to fund spending now, and use the income capacity you saved to convert traditional dollars to Roth at a pace that fits your ACA range.

Strategy A is the default for many households because it's simple: "withdraw what we need." The problem is that simplicity can be expensive when affordability hinges on income.

Strategy C can be tempting because it keeps the ACA number low, but it can leave a large traditional balance untouched, potentially setting up future tax and Medicare-related costs. (Medicare uses a different income framework for surcharges, but the broader point stands: ignoring traditional balances can shift pain into later years.)

Strategy B is not always feasible, but it's a useful target: spend from sources that don't inflate AGI too fast, then convert intentionally.

The hidden trap: paying conversion tax from the IRA itself

Many people pay the tax on a conversion by withholding or pulling extra money from the IRA. That can be convenient, but it has two ACA-adjacent downsides:

- The extra IRA distribution used to pay the tax can raise AGI further, shrinking assistance more than you expected.
- If you're under $59\frac{1}{2}$, additional penalties may apply in some cases (not an ACA issue, but a real one).

The cleaner version, when possible, is paying the conversion tax from cash savings or taxable assets. That preserves the converted amount inside the Roth and can keep the income ripple more contained. It's not always possible, but it's often worth aiming for.

Basis: the Form 8606 detail that can save you from guessing

If you've ever made nondeductible contributions to a traditional IRA, you may have "basis"—money in the IRA that has already been taxed. Basis changes the taxable portion of distributions and conversions, and the IRS tracks it through Form 8606.

This matters because conversions are not always fully taxable. Traditional-to-Roth conversions are generally includible in gross income *subject to basis rules*. If you have basis, part of a conversion may be nontaxable, which means the MAGI impact can be smaller than the conversion amount.

The planning value is big: you can estimate the taxable portion of a conversion using your basis information rather than assuming "conversion amount equals income." If you don't track basis correctly, you can end up paying tax twice *and* inflating your expected MAGI impact in your own planning.

Two practical moves help here:

- Make sure your historical nondeductible IRA contributions were reported and basis is accurate.
- Before doing a large conversion plan, confirm how much of each conversion will be taxable under the Form 8606 rules.

This is not trivia. It's the difference between steering with a speedometer and steering by vibes.

Sequencing in real life: the "two-engine" approach

A workable approach for many households is to run two engines at once:

- *Engine 1 (spending)*: fund your lifestyle from cash, high-basis taxable sales, and qualified Roth withdrawals as needed to keep your day-to-day life stable.
- *Engine 2 (conversion)*: convert a planned amount from traditional to Roth, sized to land your ACA MAGI where you want it.

This keeps spending decisions from being hijacked by conversion goals. You don't want to skip a necessary home repair because "it might raise MAGI," and you also don't want to abandon all conversion planning because "we needed cash." The two-engine approach separates those jobs.

It also creates a natural pause button. If the year becomes unexpectedly income-heavy (a surprise fund distribution, consulting work you didn't expect, a large gain you couldn't avoid), you can reduce or stop conversions without disrupting spending.

The "conversion window" and why it isn't the same every year

People sometimes search for "the right conversion amount" as if it's a permanent setting. In ACA years, the right conversion amount is usually a moving target because your income components move.

One year might have:

- unusually low dividends,
- no large gains,
- and a hefty cash cushion.

That year can support more conversion.

Another year might have:

- an inherited IRA distribution,
- a large taxable rebalance,
- or a spouse returning to work.

That year may support little or no conversion if keeping ACA MAGI in range is important.

This is why pacing conversions during the year can be safer than doing them all at once. It turns the conversion from a single high-stakes decision into a controlled process.

Don't optimize only one thing

Conversions tempt people into single-metric thinking. Tax planners want to minimize lifetime taxes. ACA planners want to maximize affordability. Investors want to keep assets invested. Real households want to sleep.

A good withdrawal plan makes peace with trade-offs. Sometimes you will accept a smaller conversion than your tax model suggests because the affordability hit is too large. Sometimes you will accept a larger conversion than your affordability model likes because reducing future traditional balances is worth it and you have a buffer. The point is that you are choosing, not stumbling.

The best plans also preserve optionality. Keeping a meaningful Roth balance, maintaining a cash reserve, and holding some taxable assets with high basis gives you multiple ways to fund spending without forcing a specific income outcome. That optionality is what makes the pre-65 window manageable.

A simple annual workflow that keeps conversions from running your life

A practical routine can keep Roth conversions in the "useful tool" category:

- *Early in the year*: estimate baseline income and decide how you'll fund spending (which assets, roughly how much).
- *Midyear*: update the estimate with actual dividends, interest, and any realized gains; decide whether conversion room is shrinking or expanding.
- *Late year*: convert only what fits after accounting for what actually happened, not what you hoped would happen.

The aim is not to micromanage. The aim is to avoid the classic mistake: doing a large conversion in December and then discovering you also had an unexpected taxable distribution, pushing the year's ACA MAGI higher than intended.

Roth conversions are a gift precisely because they're elective. Treat "elective" as a superpower. Use it to keep both your tax plan and your health coverage plan in the same room, talking to each other, instead of taking turns wrecking the other one.

Chapter 4

Choosing the Right Plan and Comparing Coverage Paths

A health plan can look cheap until you actually use it. This chapter teaches readers to shop the way smart retirees live: by comparing not just premiums, but the full financial picture, the doctors and prescriptions that matter, and the backup coverage paths that can quietly save—or cost—thousands.

4.1 Comparing Plans by Total Cost, Not Premium Alone

Marketplace shopping gets dramatically easier once you stop asking, "Which plan has the lowest monthly premium?" and start asking, "What will this plan cost us over a whole year *in the kinds of years we actually have*?" The first question is a sticker. The second is a budget.

Premiums are the part you see every month, so they get all the emotional attention. But premiums are only the entry fee. The real money often shows up later in the form of deductibles, copays, coinsurance, and the out-of-pocket maximum. Early retirees are especially vulnerable to getting misled by the premium because (1) you may be working hard to manage MAGI to earn premium tax credits, and (2) you may have the time and flexibility to chase a "good deal" that turns into an expensive surprise in March.

A better approach is to price each plan the way you'd price a car: not by the monthly payment, but by the total cost of owning it under different driving patterns. That means running three quick "usage" scenarios—a calm year, a busy year, and a bad year—and then making sure the worst-case doesn't wreck your finances or your sleep.

Step 1: Turn every plan into two numbers

For each plan, write down two anchors (both are on the Summary of Benefits and Coverage, and both matter more than the marketing name of the plan):

- *Net premium for the year*: your monthly premium *after* premium tax credits, multiplied by 12.
- *Out-of-pocket maximum* (*OOP max*): the most you should pay in a year for *covered, in-network* essential health benefits, not counting premiums.

That "not counting premiums" clause is the single most common planning mistake. People hear "maximum" and their brain relaxes. But the plan can still be expensive in a catastrophe, because a catastrophe is "premium + OOP max," not merely the OOP max.

Also note the fine print hiding in plain sight: the OOP max only protects you if you play by the plan's rules. Out-of-network bills, non-covered services, balance billing, and paperwork mishaps can all punch holes in that ceiling. Those issues are real, but the starting point is still the same: get the plan's in-network math into a form you can compare.

Step 2: Build the three-year types (calm, busy, bad)

The point of scenarios isn't to predict the future. It's to stop making a decision with only one mental picture (usually "nothing bad happens") and to force a quick check against reality.

Here are three scenario templates that work well for most early retirees. You can adjust the dollar amounts to match your own patterns and local pricing, but keep the shape.

Calm year (low use): "Mostly preventive, one or two small things"

A calm year might include:

- Preventive care (often covered with 0 cost-sharing when done in-network and coded correctly).
- A couple of primary care or urgent care visits.
- Maybe a generic prescription or two.

In a calm year, the plan's deductible often doesn't matter much; your premium dominates the total cost. This is where Bronze plans can look unbeatable. The trap is assuming this is the *only* year type worth planning for.

Busy year (moderate use): "Testing, imaging, referrals, maybe a procedure"

A busy year has enough medical activity to interact with the deductible:

- A specialist workup.
- Imaging (MRI/CT), outpatient procedure, physical therapy.
- A brand-name drug or two.

This is the year type that exposes the truth about a plan's cost-sharing design. Two plans with similar premiums can behave completely differently once you bump into the deductible and coinsurance. Busy-year math is where "cheap premium" plans often lose their crown.

Bad year (high use): "Hospital, surgery, cancer, or a serious flare"

A bad year means you're no longer shopping; you're a patient. Financially, that often means you're headed toward the OOP max. The practical question isn't "Will we hit it?" but "If we do, what's the all-in damage?"

The bad-year scenario is not pessimism. It's a structural fact about insurance: you buy it in case your year turns into a story you never wanted to tell.

Step 3: Estimate out-of-pocket spending under each scenario

Now comes the part that sounds like math but is mostly common sense: estimate what you'd pay out of pocket under each scenario *for covered, in-network care.* You don't need to perfectly model every copay. You need a reasonable estimate that is consistent across plans.

A few rules of thumb that keep the estimate honest:

- *Preventive care can be "free" and still lead to bills.* Preventive services are often covered at 0, but follow-up testing, diagnostic imaging, and specialist visits may not be. The difference between "screening" and "diagnostic" is a billing code, and the billing code drives who pays.
- *Deductible is not the same as OOP max.* Many plans have coinsurance after the deductible, so you can pay well beyond the deductible before you hit the OOP max.
- *Some services have copays before the deductible; some don't.* A plan might offer a 40 primary care visit copay even before you meet the deductible, while imaging is "deductible then coinsurance." This is why a plan with a scary deductible can still be tolerable in a calm year, and why that same plan can become brutal in a busy year.
- *Prescription coverage can be its own universe.* Some plans fold prescriptions into the medical deductible; others have separate

drug deductibles or tiered copays. For scenario planning, it's fine to fold prescriptions into a single out-of-pocket estimate as long as you're consistent and not ignoring them.

If you want one simplifying move: treat the busy year as "we pay a meaningful chunk of the deductible plus some coinsurance," and treat the bad year as "we get close to the OOP max." Your goal is not actuarial precision; your goal is making sure you're not choosing a plan based on an unrealistic year.

Step 4: Compare plans by (1) expected total cost and (2) maximum downside

For each plan and each scenario, compute:

$$\textit{Expected annual total cost} = \textit{Net annual premium} + \textit{Estimated out-of-pocket}$$

and separately:

$$\textit{Worst-case annual cost} = \textit{Net annual premium} + \textit{OOP max}$$

That's it. Two lines of math. And you've just forced every plan to answer the same question: "How expensive are you in the year I hope for, the year I can imagine, and the year I fear?"

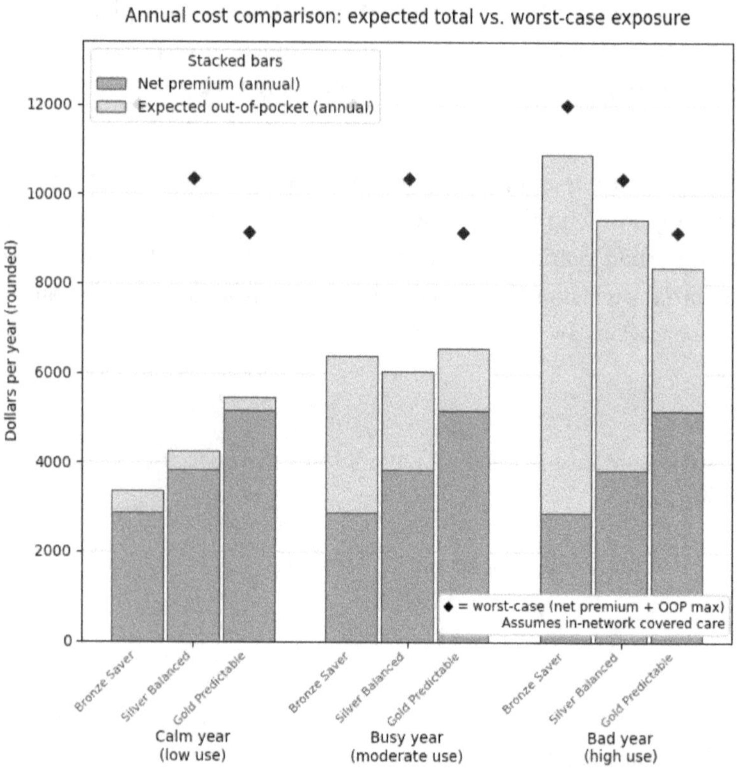

A few patterns worth noticing (before you fall in love with a premium)

Once you do even a rough three-scenario comparison, a handful of patterns tend to jump off the page.

Pattern 1: The cheapest premium often wins only in the calm year. This isn't a criticism of Bronze plans. It's just what they're built to do: trade routine predictability for a lower entry fee. If you're genuinely unlikely to use much care and you have the reserves to handle a rough year, that trade can be rational. The mistake is accidentally buying that trade without noticing you bought it.

Pattern 2: A plan can be "expensive" and still be the budget-friendly choice. Gold plans can look overpriced when you focus on premiums alone. But if you're living in the busy-year world—regular specialists, imaging, ongoing therapy, medications that aren't always cheap—the lower deductible and better cost-sharing can more than repay the higher premium. You're not buying "Gold." You're buying fewer surprises.

Pattern 3: Worst-case exposure is a planning number, not a scare tactic. A bad year has two costs: the medical problem and the financial hit. Your job is to keep the second from making the first worse. If one plan's worst-case is $5,000 higher than another's, that difference is not theoretical; it's the amount of liquidity you may need on short notice. It can influence which accounts you draw from, whether you delay realizing income, and how aggressively you can manage MAGI without cornering yourself.

Pattern 4: "We'll just be careful" is not a plan. You can be careful and still get appendicitis. You can eat perfectly and still get cancer. Insurance is not a morality play. It's a financial instrument for events that don't request your permission.

A worksheet mindset that takes 15 minutes, not 15 hours

The most dangerous plan-shopping habit is infinite research without a decision framework. The cure is a simple worksheet mindset: write down the same handful of numbers for each plan, run the same three scenarios, and then decide based on total annual cost and risk.

A compact worksheet that works well in practice:

Plan (one row per plan)	*Calm year total*	*Busy year total*	*Worst-case total*
Net annual premium	(*same number across scenarios*)		
Estimated out-of-pocket	*calm estimate*	*busy estimate*	*use OOP max*
Total annual cost	*premium + calm OOP*	*premium + busy OOP*	*premium + OOP max*

Keep it deliberately crude. Your goal isn't to guess the future down to the dollar; it's to avoid being wrong in the same direction every time (optimistic on usage, optimistic on networks, optimistic on prescriptions, optimistic on paperwork).

How to choose when the "winner" changes by scenario

Sometimes one plan is cheapest in all three scenarios. That's a gift. More often, the lowest-cost plan depends on what kind of year you have. Then you're making a choice about risk transfer, not shopping prowess.

Here's a practical way to break the tie without turning it into a philosophy seminar:

- *If calm-year savings are modest but worst-case differences are large, lean toward protection.* Saving $600 in a calm year is nice; avoiding an extra $5,000 in a bad year can preserve your flexibility (and keep you from generating unwanted income just to pay medical bills).
- *If worst-case differences are small but premiums differ a lot, lean toward the cheaper premium.* Sometimes plans converge near the OOP max, and the only real difference is the monthly price. In that situation, paying for "richer" coverage may not buy much.
- *If you already know you're in a busy-year season of life, stop pretending the calm-year scenario is your base case.* A year with planned surgery, ongoing infusions, or a known specialist-heavy con-

dition is not the time to gamble on "maybe we won't use it." Buy for the year you're actually going to live.

And there's one more tie-breaker that rarely gets written down but matters: *administrative stamina*. High-deductible designs can be perfectly rational on paper, but they demand more from you: tracking bills, questioning coding, comparing facilities, verifying coverage. If you enjoy that game, fine. If you're exhausted by it, price in the mental cost honestly. A plan that costs a bit more but runs smoothly can be worth it, especially during years that are already medically demanding.

The final check: can you actually pay the bad-year number?

Early retirement planning often treats expenses as smooth and predictable. Healthcare is the opposite: lumpy, urgent, and occasionally absurd. Before you enroll, do one last gut-check:

- If you had to pay the plan's worst-case total over 3–6 months, where would the money come from?
- Would paying it force you to realize extra income that breaks your subsidy planning?
- Would it force you to sell investments at a bad time?

If the answer is "we'd figure it out," that's not a plan—it's a hope with a billing department attached. A plan with a slightly higher premium but a significantly lower worst-case may be doing something very valuable: turning a financial emergency into an inconvenience.

A practical plan-selection checklist (total cost edition)

Use this to make a clean decision without drowning in details:

1. Write down each plan's *net annual premium* and *OOP max*.

2. Estimate out-of-pocket spending for a calm year and a busy year using the same assumptions across plans.
3. Compute three totals for each plan: calm-year total, busy-year total, worst-case total.
4. Circle the plan that best matches the year you're most likely to have, then confirm you can afford the worst-case total without blowing up your broader financial plan.
5. Only after the math works, allow yourself to care about the monthly premium.

Premium is what you pay to stay in the game. Total cost is what the game costs you. When you compare plans on total cost—with a calm year, a busy year, and a bad year on the table—you stop shopping for a product and start buying a strategy.

4.2 Networks, Specialists, and Prescription Drug Reality Checks

A Marketplace plan can win your spreadsheet and still lose your real life. The usual culprit isn't the deductible or the metal tier. It's the mundane stuff: your doctor isn't actually in-network, the "in-network" hospital uses an out-of-network physician group for something routine, the plan requires referrals for everything, or your maintenance medication sits on a tier that quietly turns $30/month into "call us to discuss options."

Treat plan shopping like booking a nonrefundable trip for a whole year of your health. You wouldn't glance at the hotel price and assume the flight exists. You'd confirm the flight, the dates, the baggage rules, and whether the airport is three hours from the actual city. Networks and drug coverage are that "airport three hours away" problem: the plan can be technically valid and practically unusable.

The network is the plan (the premium is just the cover charge)

"Network" sounds like a boring administrative detail until it becomes a financial event. Network participation is a major hidden driver of cost: in-network care generally costs less; out-of-network care may be not covered or covered at much worse terms depending on plan type. That's the polite version. The blunt version is: some Marketplace plans are designed so that out-of-network is basically "you're on your own" unless it's a true emergency.

And narrow networks are common in the ACA Marketplace. That's not a conspiracy; it's a pricing strategy. Insurers keep premiums down by contracting with fewer providers, negotiating harder, and steering members toward certain systems. The trade is real: a narrower network can mean lower premiums and sometimes decent in-network pricing, but it also raises the odds that a doctor or hospital you want won't be covered. A meaningful share of Marketplace enrollees report that a doctor or hospital they needed was not covered in the past year. That's not a theoretical risk; it's a lived one.

So the right mindset is skepticism with receipts. Provider directories can be wrong, outdated, or misleading. Provider offices can misunderstand which "version" of an insurer they accept. Hospitals can be in-network while the specialists working inside them are not. If you do the verification work up front, you buy yourself a year with fewer billing surprises and fewer "we need to reschedule you" phone calls.

Plan types: rules of the road matter more than the logo

Marketplace plans often show up as HMOs, EPOs, and PPOs. The letters matter less than the rules they imply:

- *HMO-ish rules* often mean: pick a primary care provider (PCP), get referrals for specialists, stay in-network or pay the full freight (except emergencies).

- *EPO-ish rules* often mean: no referrals required in many cases, but still essentially no out-of-network coverage (except emergencies).
- *PPO-ish rules* often mean: more flexibility to go out-of-network, usually at higher cost-sharing, sometimes with a separate out-of-network deductible and out-of-pocket limit.

If you're healthy and mostly want catastrophic protection, these distinctions can seem academic. If you already have a specialist you trust, or you're managing something chronic, they're operational. The plan type tells you what your day-to-day life will look like: how many calls you'll make, how many hoops you'll jump through, and how often you'll be told, "That provider isn't in your network."

One more practical detail: plan rules can be strict even when the provider is in-network. Some plans require that care be "medically necessary" by their standards, which is where prior authorization enters the picture. That brings us to the two main friction points that don't show up in premium and deductible math: referrals and prior authorization.

Referrals: the hidden calendar tax

Referrals sound harmless until you're the one coordinating them. A referral requirement means your PCP becomes the air-traffic controller for most specialist care. For some people, that's fine. For others it's a nuisance that becomes expensive in time, delays, and extra appointments.

A referral requirement can impose a "calendar tax" in a few common ways:

- You need an extra PCP visit just to obtain permission to see a specialist you already see annually.

- A specialist visit gets canceled because the referral didn't arrive, wasn't renewed, or was written for the wrong specialist group.
- You're traveling, you need care, and your PCP is now the gatekeeper from a thousand miles away.

None of those are medical problems. They're workflow problems. They're also the kind of problem that makes people overuse urgent care or delay care until something becomes acute.

If you know you'll be in and out of specialist offices, treat referral rules as a real cost. It's not a line item on your budget, but it changes your life all year.

Prior authorization: permission slips for grown-ups

Prior authorization is the insurer's "prove it" mechanism. The doctor recommends an MRI, a brand-name medication, an injection, a surgery, a sleep study, physical therapy beyond a certain number of visits—and the plan may require documentation before it agrees to pay.

Sometimes prior authorization is quick and reasonable. Sometimes it becomes a long-running side quest that drains the energy of everyone involved. The problem isn't that prior authorization exists; it's that you don't know *how much of it* you're buying until you're already enrolled.

Three ways prior authorization creates regret:

- *Delay*: The care isn't denied outright, but it's held up. If you're trying to get imaging to rule something out, delay can be its own kind of harm.
- *Substitution*: The plan pushes "step therapy" logic—try a cheaper drug first, then "fail" it, then maybe get the one your doctor chose.

- *Administrative exhaustion*: Even successful approvals can take multiple rounds of paperwork. You may spend hours on the phone just to get a claim processed the way it was supposed to be processed.

You can't eliminate this risk completely, but you can screen for it. When two plans are close on total cost, a plan with simpler specialist access and fewer restrictions can be the better value—even if the premium is higher—because it reduces the chance that you'll pay in time, stress, and delayed care.

A reality-check workflow that catches most problems before they become bills

If you only do one thing before clicking "Enroll," do this: verify your *actual* care. Not "a doctor." *Your* doctor. Not "a hospital." *The* hospital you'd actually go to. Not "prescription coverage." *Your* prescriptions.

A practical workflow:

1) Build a "non-negotiables" list

Write down:

- Your key doctors (PCP plus any specialists you'd be upset to lose).
- The hospital system you'd want in a true emergency and the one where your doctors actually admit patients.
- Any labs or imaging centers you regularly use (or that your specialists tend to send you to).
- Every maintenance medication (name, dose, and whether you can tolerate switching).

This list does two things: it prevents you from being swayed by marketing, and it makes you compare plans based on what you'll genuinely use.

2) Check the plan's provider directory (then assume it's wrong until confirmed)

Start with the plan's provider directory for each shortlisted plan. Search your specialists first, not your PCP. If a plan doesn't have your cardiologist, oncologist, rheumatologist, or other key specialist, it's not "almost right." It's wrong.

Even if you find the provider, don't stop there. Directories can show the doctor as "in-network" while the office only accepts a different product line from the same insurer, or only accepts the plan at a different location, or is no longer taking new patients.

3) Call the provider's office and ask a very specific question

The goal is not "Do you take Insurance Company X?" That question invites a confident wrong answer.

Ask: *"Do you accept this specific Marketplace plan name (and the network it uses)?"* Give them the plan name exactly as it appears, and if you have it, the network name. If the person you reach sounds unsure, ask for billing. If billing sounds unsure, ask what information they need to verify it.

This call is awkward. Do it anyway. The ten minutes of awkwardness is cheap compared to discovering midyear that "taking the insurer" didn't mean "in-network for your plan."

4) Confirm the hospital and the facility-based services you're likely to encounter

Hospitals are not one bill. They're a collection of billers: the facility, the emergency physician group, radiology, anesthesiology, pathology, labs, surgical assistants, and so on.

The No Surprises Act protections (effective Jan 1, 2022) reduce certain unexpected out-of-network bills for emergency care and some services at in-network facilities, but they don't eliminate all "network surprise" risk. It's still possible to run into out-of-network exposure in situations that don't fit neatly into the protected categories, and it's still possible to have a mess that requires follow-up, appeals, and persistence.

So rather than aiming for "guaranteed safe," aim for "lower probability of chaos":

- Prefer plans where your main hospital system is clearly in-network.
- If you have planned procedures, ask the surgeon's office which facility they use and whether that facility is in-network for your plan.
- If you have ongoing imaging, check the imaging center itself; "hospital in-network" doesn't automatically cover the outpatient imaging facility across town.

This is the unglamorous work that makes your deductible-and-premium math come true in practice.

Specialists: don't assume the hospital implies the doctor

One of the most common enrollment regrets is assuming that a respected hospital system implies broad specialist coverage. In reality, a hospital may be in-network, while a specialist group that practices there is not. Or the specialist is in-network, but only at one location, or only for existing patients, or only on certain days.

If you want a single high-impact test: take your most important specialist and search them across plans. If Plan A includes them and Plan B does not, that's not a minor detail. That's the plan telling you how it expects you to receive care.

Also watch for the "new patient" problem. A provider may be technically in-network but not accepting new patients. That turns "covered" into "unavailable," which is just a different flavor of uncovered. When you're enrolling, availability is part of coverage in the practical sense.

Prescription drugs: the formulary is the gatekeeper

Premiums get headlines. Deductibles get arguments. Prescriptions get people into trouble quietly.

Formularies are the practical gatekeeper for prescription affordability. Being on-formulary usually costs less and off-formulary drugs may require an exceptions process with physician support. That's not merely about money; it's about continuity. If a drug is off-formulary, you may be pushed into substitutions, delays, or repeated paperwork. If a drug is on-formulary but on a high tier with restrictions, you may still pay far more than you expect.

A smart drug check is simple and ruthless: look up each medication on each plan's formulary and write down four items.

1) Is it covered at all?

If it's not listed, assume it's not covered until you verify otherwise. Some plans cover the drug under a different name or a different form (tablet vs. capsule), but "not listed" is a red flag that deserves follow-up.

2) What tier is it on?

Tier placement often predicts your cost-sharing. The exact tier structure varies by plan, but the pattern is consistent: higher tiers tend to cost more and come with more restrictions.

Tier alone doesn't tell you the dollar amount, but it tells you whether the plan is treating your medication as routine, preferred, or grudgingly tolerated.

3) Does the plan apply a deductible to drugs?

Some plans make you pay the full negotiated price until you satisfy a drug deductible (or the overall deductible). Others offer copays for certain generics right away. This matters enormously for the first months of the year, when you're most likely to be paying full freight.

If you take a brand-name medication and the plan applies the deductible to it, you can end up spending a large amount early in the year even if your monthly premium is low. That's not necessarily "bad," but it needs to be intentional. It's a budgeting choice.

4) Are there restrictions? (Prior authorization / step therapy / quantity limits)

Restrictions are the difference between "covered" and "covered after a fight."

If you see prior authorization or step therapy on a medication you rely on, treat that as a real planning input. You may still choose the plan, but now you're choosing it with eyes open and you can prepare: ask your doctor's office if they've dealt with that insurer's process, and plan lead time for renewals.

Preferred pharmacies: the small print that changes the receipt

Many plans steer you to preferred pharmacies, and the price gap can be meaningful. Even if a drug is covered and on a reasonable tier, using a non-preferred pharmacy can increase your cost. Mail-order rules can also matter, especially for maintenance medications.

If you have a strong preference for one pharmacy (location, service, delivery), confirm it's preferred. If it's not, you're not just comparing plans; you're deciding whether you're willing to change your pharmacy routine for a year.

Exceptions and appeals: a safety valve, not a strategy

Plans usually have a process to request coverage for a non-formulary drug or to request an exception. Off-formulary drugs may require an exceptions process with physician support. That support can be hard to get, especially if your doctor's office is overwhelmed or isn't familiar with your new plan.

It's tempting to say, "We'll just file an exception if we need to." As a backup, yes. As a plan-selection strategy, no. Choose a plan that covers your medication cleanly if you can. Save the exception process for genuine edge cases, not predictable needs.

How to use these checks without turning plan shopping into a second job

There's a danger in becoming so thorough that you never decide. The trick is to triage.

- If you rarely use care and have no ongoing prescriptions, you can keep the verification light: confirm one good PCP option, confirm your nearest hospital is in-network, and do a quick scan for any medications you might start (for example, common generics).
- If you have chronic conditions, ongoing specialist care, planned procedures, or expensive medications, this verification *is* the work. In that case, treat it like you're protecting a major line item in your budget—which you are.

The key is honesty about your own usage. A plan that's "fine for most people" can be a terrible match for someone whose health care is specialist-driven or pharmacy-driven.

A pre-enrollment reality-check list (printable mindset)

Before enrolling, try to get to "yes" on each of the following. If you can't, at least know what you're trading away.

1. *Doctors*: My PCP and my key specialist(s) are in-network for *this exact plan*, and the offices confirm they accept it.
2. *Hospitals*: The hospital system I would actually use is in-network.
3. *Specialist access*: I understand whether referrals are required, and I'm comfortable with the practical hassle level.
4. *Prior authorization*: I know whether my likely services and medications tend to trigger prior authorization, and I'm prepared for the process.
5. *Medications*: Each maintenance medication is on-formulary; I've noted tier, deductible treatment, and restrictions.
6. *Pharmacies*: My preferred pharmacy is acceptable (ideally preferred), or I'm willing to switch.

If this checklist sounds picky, that's the point. Regret usually comes from assumptions. Assumptions are expensive.

The payoff: your "total cost" math becomes real

Total-cost comparisons are only as good as the assumptions underneath them. If your plan's network doesn't include the clinicians you'll actually see, your neat out-of-pocket estimate doesn't matter; you've wandered into a different universe where "covered" becomes "not covered," or where care gets delayed until it's more complicated and more expensive.

A plan that passes the network and prescription reality checks earns the right to be evaluated on premiums, deductibles, and out-of-pocket limits. A plan that fails them doesn't deserve more analysis. The most cost-effective plan is the one you can use without constant friction—the one that lets you spend your time enjoying your days, not negotiating your way to basic medical care.

4.3 Why Plan Prices Shift and Why Re-Shopping Matters

The most expensive Marketplace plan is often the one you *keep*.

Not because you made a foolish choice last year. Not because you missed some secret "best plan" page. It's expensive for the same reason a great grocery store deal disappears: the store changes prices, the competitors change prices, and the coupon in your hand is pegged to a specific item that might not be the same item next week.

Marketplace pricing behaves like that. Premiums move. Networks and formularies get revised. Carriers enter and exit counties. And the subsidy math is anchored to a local benchmark that can change from year to year. Put all of that together and the value leaderboard gets reshuffled—sometimes gently, sometimes violently.

Premium changes can be significant from one plan year to the next; analyses of preliminary filings show insurers may propose material increases and cite multiple drivers (medical cost trend and policy/-market uncertainty). That's the market speaking in its own language. Your job isn't to become fluent in filings and actuarial memos. Your job is to build the habit that makes those changes less expensive to you: re-shop every year with a fresh set of eyes.

Why last year's winner can become this year's overpay

A plan's premium is not a stable personality trait. It's a price set in a competitive environment that changes all the time. A carrier that priced aggressively to gain membership might decide it's grown enough and raise rates. A carrier that lost membership might sharpen its pencil. A new carrier might enter your area and shake things up. A large hospital system might renegotiate contracts, changing the carrier's underlying costs.

Insurer participation changes (e.g., fewer insurers in some states/areas) can reduce competition, alter networks, and change premium levels and plan availability. This is the part shoppers feel most viscerally: fewer logos on the screen, fewer plan options that include the doctors you want, and a sudden sense that the "same plan" is simply priced higher. Sometimes it is. Sometimes it's also narrower or more restrictive in ways that won't show up until you need care.

There's another quiet driver that has nothing to do with your county's competitive drama: annual updates to federal parameters. Even if premiums were stable, annual updates to federal parameters (like the maximum annual limitation on cost sharing) can shift the total financial risk profile. Translation: the legal ceiling on out-of-pocket exposure can move, and plans can move with it. A plan may "look the same" in the brochure while your worst-case number creeps up.

So if your plan auto-renews and you never re-open the shopping screen, you're implicitly betting that:

- your carrier stayed competitively priced,
- your doctors and hospitals stayed in-network,
- your drugs stayed on the formulary in a friendly tier,
- the benchmark and subsidy dynamics stayed aligned with your plan,
- the plan's cost-sharing didn't tilt in a way that matters for your health profile.

That's a lot of bets for a decision you didn't actively make.

The moving anchor: why the benchmark matters even if you don't buy it

As we saw, the benchmark plan is the anchor that helps determine how large your premium tax credits can be. What matters here is not the definition; it's the consequence: your subsidy is tethered to the price of a specific local plan that may change each year.

Benchmark dynamics matter: competitive positioning relative to the benchmark (second-lowest-cost silver) affects enrollment and can influence how aggressively insurers price plans. This creates a strange consumer reality: your subsidy can change substantially even if your income stays steady, simply because the benchmark moved.

Think about what that means. If the benchmark premium rises, subsidies can rise too (subject to the rules tied to your household's situation). That can make *many* plans cheaper after subsidy, including plans you weren't considering. If the benchmark premium falls, subsidies can shrink, and the plan you kept might suddenly cost much more per month with no change to your medical needs.

This is why a plan's *gross* premium (before subsidy) is a misleading way to shop, and why a plan's *net* premium (after subsidy) must be refreshed every year. A plan can keep the same gross premium and still become "more expensive" to you because the benchmark moved underneath it.

Silver loading: the reason prices can look upside down

One of the oddest Marketplace experiences is seeing a Gold plan priced close to a Silver plan, or a Bronze plan that seems too good to be true after subsidies. That's not your imagination. It's often tied to a pricing phenomenon commonly called "silver loading."

Here's the shopper's version, stripped of legal backstory: in many places, insurers concentrate certain costs into Silver plan premiums. When that happens, Silver premiums can become inflated relative to Bronze and Gold. Since premium tax credits are tied to the benchmark Silver plan, a higher Silver premium can raise the subsidy amount. And that larger subsidy can spill over to make Bronze or Gold plans unusually attractive after the subsidy is applied.

So you can get a year where:

- a Bronze plan becomes extremely cheap after subsidy (sometimes shockingly cheap),
- a Gold plan is only modestly more expensive than Silver, while offering lower cost-sharing.

The key lesson isn't to chase any specific metal tier. The lesson is that the market can tilt. The best value can rotate. If you don't re-shop, you'll miss the year where the tilt favors you.

Why "auto-renew" is a financial decision in disguise

Auto-renew feels safe. You keep your member ID card, you avoid decision fatigue, and you don't risk accidentally picking the wrong plan. But auto-renew is also a choice to accept whatever price and design changes your plan brings into the new year.

The "trap" is subtle: auto-renew often preserves continuity, but it doesn't preserve competitiveness. Your plan may no longer be the best match for your expected healthcare use or your risk tolerance. It may no longer be the best match for your MAGI plan. It may have quietly changed the way it handles prescriptions, imaging, specialist visits, or referrals.

And auto-renew has a second hidden cost: it can keep you from noticing the year when a small amount of shopping work would buy a large benefit. The Marketplace is lever-rich, but only for those who pull the levers.

Re-shopping isn't disloyalty; it's routine maintenance

In other parts of your finances, you already do this. You check interest rates. You review your asset allocation. You re-bid insurance every so often. Health plans deserve the same treatment, except the schedule is non-negotiable: the whole Marketplace resets annually.

Re-shopping doesn't have to mean switching. Sometimes the best decision is to stay put. The point is that staying should be the outcome of a comparison, not the default caused by inertia.

The five numbers and two "gotchas" that should be re-checked annually

If you want a re-shopping habit that's thorough without being miserable, focus on a small set of inputs that drive most of the financial outcome.

Five numbers

1. *Net premium (monthly and annual)*: after your subsidy estimate for the new year.
2. *Medical deductible*: and whether key services are subject to it.
3. *Prescription deductible*: if separate, and whether common generics are exempt.
4. *Out-of-pocket maximum*: your worst-case exposure for covered in-network care (premiums still separate, as we saw).
5. *Primary care and specialist visit cost-sharing*: not because office visits are the big-ticket item, but because the structure hints at how "high-deductible" the plan feels in daily life.

Those five numbers usually tell you whether the plan is leaning toward "cheap entry fee, expensive usage" or "higher premium, smoother usage."

Two gotchas that cause real regret

- *Network changes*: a plan can keep the same name while dropping a hospital system or a specialist group. Insurer participation changes can also force you to pick from narrower options.
- *Formulary changes*: a drug that was on a friendly tier can move, gain restrictions, or be treated differently under the deductible. If you rely on certain medications, this is not a footnote; it's the plan.

The unpleasant truth: the more your health care involves specialists and prescriptions, the more re-shopping matters. A plan that's "good enough" for someone who sees a doctor twice a year can be a constant source of friction for someone managing chronic conditions.

A consumer-friendly explanation of why premiums jump

It's natural to want a single culprit when a premium rises: "My insurer is greedy," or "Healthcare is broken," or "The government changed something." In reality, there are multiple overlapping drivers, and you don't need to adjudicate them to protect your budget.

Premium changes can be significant from one plan year to the next; analyses of preliminary filings show insurers may propose material increases and cite multiple drivers (medical cost trend and policy/-market uncertainty). The parts you can translate into shopper terms are:

- *Medical cost trend*: care gets more expensive, negotiated rates change, drug costs shift, utilization changes.
- *Market uncertainty*: carrier strategy responds to who's enrolling, how sick the pool is, and expectations about future rules.

- *Local competition*: one carrier leaving or entering can swing pricing across the whole menu.

The takeaway isn't cynicism. It's pattern recognition. Premiums aren't a verdict on you. They're a moving price in a moving market. Your defense is shopping.

Why re-shopping can improve coverage without increasing the net premium

The best re-shopping outcomes often aren't "save $30 a month." They're "pay roughly the same, but buy a plan that behaves better."

Re-shopping can sometimes uncover:

- a Gold plan priced close to Silver after subsidy (a silver loading year can create this),
- a plan with a lower out-of-pocket maximum for a modest net premium increase,
- a plan with meaningfully better prescription terms,
- a plan that includes the hospital system you'd actually use.

That's why a pure premium-focused re-shop is too narrow. The goal is to re-run the total-cost comparison mindset with this year's prices, and to overlay the network and formulary checks that keep the math from turning into fantasy.

A simple annual re-shopping ritual that doesn't eat your life

The ritual matters more than the perfection.

1. *Pick a shortlist*: your current plan plus two or three plausible alternatives (often one cheaper, one middle, one richer).
2. *Refresh the net premiums*: use the new year's subsidy estimate rather than last year's memory.

3. *Re-run your three usage scenarios*: calm, busy, bad. Keep the assumptions the same so you're comparing the plans, not your mood.
4. *Do quick network and drug spot-checks*: your key doctors, your main hospital, and your maintenance meds.
5. *Decide actively*: stay or switch, but make it a choice you could defend in two sentences.

If you do only that, you'll avoid the most common way people overpay: sleepwalking into a plan year that no longer fits.

The quiet benefit: re-shopping protects your broader financial plan

Health coverage in the gap years isn't just a health decision; it's a planning decision. A plan with a lower worst-case exposure can reduce the odds you'll need to generate extra income at an inconvenient time. A plan with better drug coverage can reduce month-to-month volatility. A plan with a stable network can reduce the time you spend fighting bills and chasing authorizations, freeing you up for the parts of your life you actually retired for.

And perhaps most importantly: re-shopping keeps you in control. It turns the Marketplace from a once—a-year ambush into a once—a-year tune-up. The prices will keep moving. The benchmark will keep shifting. Carriers will keep adjusting. The only sustainable move is to expect that—and to shop accordingly.

4.4 HSAs in the Gap Years and Near Medicare

An HSA is the rare financial tool that behaves like it was designed by someone who actually retires early. It can lower your current-year tax bill, grow quietly in the background, and later pay for a category of spending that tends to be stubbornly non-optional. In the gap years, that combination is potent: health costs are real, subsidies are sensitive to income, and flexibility is worth more than bragging rights.

But HSAs have a personality. They reward precision and punish autopilot. The same account that can function as a tax-sheltered medical reserve can also turn into a paperwork-and-penalty headache if you contribute when you're not eligible—especially as Medicare approaches and the rules get trickier than most people expect.

HSA basics that matter in practice (not brochure copy)

Most people know the headline: contribute pre-tax, invest, spend on qualified medical expenses tax-free. What actually matters for planning is how an HSA behaves across time:

- *It's a medical sinking fund that can compound.* You can keep money invested for years, then draw it out for qualified medical expenses later.
- *It can smooth lumpy healthcare years.* If you choose a plan with a higher deductible, the HSA can be the buffer that keeps January from turning into a financial scramble.
- *It plays nicely with income management.* Paying medical bills from an HSA doesn't create taxable income. In a year where you're trying to keep MAGI in a particular range, that can matter.

The HSA is not automatically *best*. It's best when it matches the rest of your situation: your health needs, your tolerance for variable out-of-pocket spending, and your ability to keep a cash-like cushion available.

Eligibility is the gate: the HSA is only as good as the plan attached to it

HSAs aren't available just because you want one. To contribute, you must be covered by an HSA-qualified high-deductible health plan

(HDHP) and meet the other eligibility rules. The rule that sneaks up on people in their 60s is simple and absolute:

> HSA contribution eligibility requires (among other rules) not being enrolled in Medicare.

That sentence should change how you think about the last stretch before Medicare. Your HSA doesn't end at 65. Your ability to *contribute* ends when Medicare begins. And "begins" can be more complicated than the day you think you enrolled.

Why an HSA can be a smart gap-years medical reserve

If you're in the gap years with reasonably good health and a plan that makes HSA contributions possible, the HSA can serve three distinct roles. You can use one, two, or all three, depending on temperament.

Role 1: The deductible shock absorber

High deductibles are psychologically irritating. Even if you can afford them, it's annoying to see a big bill early in the year. An HSA turns that irritation into something closer to a routine transfer: the money was already earmarked.

In a calm year, the HSA may hardly get used. In a busy year, it may function exactly like insurance *should* function: not eliminating costs, but making costs survivable without forcing you to rearrange your entire financial life.

Role 2: The "receipts strategy" (using time as a tax advantage)

One of the most underrated HSA features is that you can pay qualified medical expenses out of pocket today, save the receipts, and reimburse yourself from the HSA later. That converts today's medical spending into a future pool of tax-free withdrawals you can take at a time of your choosing.

In the gap years, that "time-shift" can be useful if you're carefully managing income. You can treat accumulated receipts as a kind of emergency lever: if you need extra spending money later without increasing taxable income, you reimburse yourself. You're not gaming the system; you're using the system as designed.

The catch is behavioral: it requires recordkeeping and the patience to leave the HSA invested. Some people love this. Others would rather simplify their life and just use the HSA as intended in real time. Both can be rational.

Role 3: A Medicare-era medical reserve

Even after you stop contributing, the HSA can still pay for qualified medical expenses. Healthcare spending doesn't stop at 65; it usually changes shape. The HSA can become the dedicated pool that pays for copays, dental work, vision expenses, and other qualified costs that don't politely vanish once Medicare shows up.

This is the part many people miss: the "gap years HSA" can be the "first years of Medicare HSA," too. The account doesn't expire. The eligibility to add fresh money is what has a hard stop.

The non-obvious trade-off: an HSA plan is not always the cheapest plan

An HSA-qualified HDHP can be a great deal, but it can also be a mirage if you buy it for the tax perk and then discover the plan design doesn't fit your healthcare reality.

A common mistake is forcing an HSA plan onto a year that's likely to be medically busy. The tax benefit of contributing may be smaller than the extra out-of-pocket cost you absorb through a higher deductible and higher coinsurance. In other words, you save a little on taxes and spend a lot on medical bills. That's not strategy; that's an expensive hobby.

The simplest way to avoid that mistake is to treat the HSA plan like any other plan: run the calm/busy/bad year totals, and then layer the HSA value on top. If the HSA plan is already competitive on total cost, the tax advantage is a bonus. If it's not competitive, the tax advantage is unlikely to rescue it.

Contribution timing: the HSA rewards clean edges

HSAs are deceptively sensitive to timing. You can contribute monthly, you can contribute in a lump sum, you can contribute late in the year. This flexibility is great for people whose income varies, or who want to wait until they're sure they're eligible.

But the flexibility cuts both ways: it makes it easy to accidentally contribute when you shouldn't—especially around Medicare.

If you're approaching 65, treat your HSA contributions like you treat an automatic bill pay for a credit card you plan to close: turn it off early and deliberately. The cost of turning it off "too soon" is a slightly smaller contribution. The cost of turning it off "too late" can be an excess contribution problem that requires corrections and paperwork.

Medicare Part A retroactivity: the trapdoor near age 65

Here's the rule that catches careful people, not careless ones:

> If a consumer delays applying for Medicare and later enrolls, Medicare Part A can be retroactive (SSA notes up to 6 months for those over 65), which can retroactively make HSA contributions for those months 'excess' contributions.

Read that again slowly. It means you can do everything "right" according to your calendar and still end up "wrong" according to Medicare's retroactive coverage start.

A typical scenario looks like this:

- You turn 65 and keep working your plan: stay on an HSA-qualified HDHP, keep contributing, and delay Medicare because you're not ready to switch.
- Later, you apply for Medicare Part A.
- Part A is backdated (up to six months for those over 65, per SSA guidance).
- Suddenly, you were "enrolled in Medicare" for months you thought you weren't, which can retroactively make your HSA contributions for those months excess contributions.

This isn't a loophole; it's a trapdoor. It's also why the phrase "not enrolled in Medicare" matters more than "not paying for Medicare".

A practical "final contribution month" mindset

To handle the retroactivity risk, adopt a mindset that feels conservative but prevents headaches:

- Decide approximately when you'll apply for Medicare.
- Count backward and stop HSA contributions sufficiently early to avoid the window that could become retroactively covered by Part A.

The exact best timing depends on your situation, and you'll want to be precise with your own enrollment plan. The point here is the planning posture: *stop contributions before the application, not after the enrollment confirmation arrives*. The retroactive feature makes "after" an unreliable concept.

This is also where payroll deductions can create accidental contributions. If you have any automatic HSA contributions—from an employer, from a monthly bank transfer, or from a habit you set years ago—treat that automation as guilty until proven turned off. Medicare doesn't care that the contribution was "automatic."

What happens if you accidentally contribute too long?

Mistakes happen. The important part is not panicking and not ignoring it.

IRS Pub 969 describes the tax consequences and correction rules for excess HSA contributions (including timing-sensitive removal to avoid ongoing excise tax). The details matter, and they're timing-sensitive. Conceptually, the remedy involves identifying the excess amount (and any associated earnings) and correcting it according to the IRS-described process and deadlines.

Two practical observations, without pretending the paperwork is fun:

- *The sooner you catch it, the cleaner the fix tends to be.* Waiting can compound the administrative mess.
- *Keep documentation.* If Part A was backdated and you correct contributions, you want a clean paper trail that matches the dates.

If you're anywhere near Medicare age and still contributing, a quick annual check should become routine: "Are we still eligible to contribute, and are we in a window where retroactive Part A could reach back into our contribution months?"

Choosing between "spend from the HSA now" and "save receipts for later"

People get oddly moral about this choice, as though one option is disciplined and the other is indulgent. It's not moral. It's tactical.

Reasons to spend from the HSA now

- You want simplicity and fewer files to track.

- You prefer certainty: pay the bill, reimburse immediately, move on.
- Your portfolio plan doesn't hinge on maximizing tax-advantaged space.

Spending from the HSA now can be perfectly wise. The "best" strategy is the one you'll actually execute correctly for years.

Reasons to save receipts and reimburse later

- You can comfortably pay medical bills out of pocket and want to keep the HSA invested.
- You value the option to create tax-free spending later, especially in years you're carefully managing income.
- You like having a dedicated "break glass" lever that doesn't trigger additional taxable income.

The receipts strategy is powerful, but it's only as good as your record-keeping. A shoebox of fading pharmacy receipts is not a strategy; it's future frustration.

Coordinating an HSA with Marketplace coverage: the "two good reasons" test

Some people try to contort their Marketplace plan choice to preserve HSA eligibility. Sometimes that's smart. Sometimes it's reverse-engineering the answer.

A clean decision rule is the "two good reasons" test:

- *Reason one: the plan itself is a good fit.* It works under your calm/busy/bad year totals, and it passes the network and formulary reality checks.

- *Reason two: you will actually use the HSA advantage.* You'll contribute meaningfully, and you have a plan for using or investing the funds.

If you only have one good reason ("I like HSAs"), you're at risk of buying a plan that doesn't serve you medically or financially.

The "turn 65 soon" example that prevents most HSA mistakes

Consider someone who turns 65 in the middle of next year and plans to apply for Medicare after wrapping up a few commitments. They want to keep an HSA-qualified HDHP as long as possible and keep contributing, because the tax benefit is real.

The planning move that saves them is not complicated: they stop HSA contributions months before they apply for Medicare, specifically because Part A may be backdated. They document their last eligible contribution month, stop any automatic contributions, and keep that record with their tax documents.

This approach is boring. That's why it works. HSA problems near Medicare are rarely about misunderstanding what an HSA is. They're about underestimating how unforgiving the timing rules can be.

When an HSA is not worth forcing

HSAs are popular enough that people sometimes treat them as a badge of financial competence. That's a mistake. The "right" plan is the one that fits your actual healthcare usage, your budget, and your stress tolerance.

An HSA-qualified HDHP can be the wrong tool when:

- your healthcare needs are predictably heavy and the plan's cost-sharing is likely to be expensive year after year,

- the network is too narrow for your specialists and the hassle cost will be high,
- you're close enough to Medicare that contribution timing becomes a recurring risk, and the incremental tax benefit is small relative to the potential for excess-contribution cleanup.

Sometimes the best decision is to use the gap years to simplify: pick a plan that behaves well in your likely scenario, and treat the HSA as optional rather than essential.

A clean operating rule for the last stretch before Medicare

If you want a single rule that prevents the most common Medicare-adjacent HSA mistake, it's this:

> Don't make HSA contributions in any month that could later be treated as Medicare enrollment month due to retroactive Part A.

That rule naturally pushes you toward conservative timing, which is exactly what you want. The financial upside of squeezing in one more month of contributions is usually modest. The downside of discovering you contributed during months that are retroactively covered by Medicare is disproportionately annoying.

HSAs can be a cornerstone tool in the gap years: a tax-friendly medical reserve that gives you options and reduces the chance that a healthcare year forces an unwanted financial move. Near Medicare, the same tool demands better boundaries. Treat eligibility like a hard gate, treat timing like a sharp edge, and the HSA remains what it's supposed to be: helpful, flexible, and quietly powerful.

4.5 COBRA, Employer Offers, and Spouse Coverage Trade-Offs

The most stressful moment in gap-years healthcare is rarely open enrollment. It's the Tuesday afternoon when your old coverage ends Friday, you're still processing the life change that caused it, and two very official-sounding options sit in front of you: "Take COBRA" or "Go to the Marketplace." One option looks like continuity and safety. The other looks like paperwork and uncertainty.

That instinct—pay for what you know—isn't irrational. It's also expensive surprisingly often. The smart move is to treat coverage paths like a bridge choice, not a loyalty test. You're trying to get from "employer plan world" to "Medicare world" with the fewest financial potholes and the least medical disruption. Sometimes COBRA is the right bridge. Sometimes the Marketplace is. Sometimes the best answer is "split the bridge" over time.

COBRA in plain English: you keep the plan, you pay the whole bill

COBRA generally applies to employers with 20+ employees and can require paying up to 102% of the plan cost, making it expensive but potentially valuable for continuity of care (network) and near-term simplicity. That sentence contains the whole trade.

Continuity is the obvious benefit. Same plan. Same network. Same rules for prior authorization. Often the same deductibles and out-of-pocket tracking for the rest of the plan year. If you're in the middle of treatment, that can be priceless.

The whole bill is the part people underestimate. While employed, you saw only your share of the premium. Under COBRA, you may be picking up both your share and the employer's share, plus a small administrative add-on. The sticker shock isn't a sign you're being punished; it's the true price of the plan that was partially hidden before.

COBRA also has an emotional advantage: speed. When you're rushed, "keep what you have" is a powerful default. The danger is letting that default run for months or years without checking whether it still makes sense.

The four reasons COBRA can be worth the money

COBRA is not automatically bad. It's simply expensive, so it has to earn its keep. Here are the situations where it often does.

1) You're mid-year and you've already paid a lot toward the deductible or out-of-pocket maximum

This is the most concrete reason. Employer plans track your deductible and out-of-pocket spending across the plan year. COBRA typically continues that same plan and those same accumulators. Switching to a Marketplace plan mid-year usually means starting over at $0 on the deductible and out-of-pocket maximum.

So if you've already had a busy medical year, COBRA can be a financial bargain *despite* the premium. You're buying your way out of paying the same deductible twice.

This is the kind of analysis that rewards a quick calculation:

- How much deductible/OOP have we already satisfied this year?
- How much more care is likely before December 31?
- What would a new plan's deductible reset cost us?

If you're likely to hit the out-of-pocket maximum under the employer plan anyway, COBRA can be the "pay the premium, avoid restarting the meter" option.

2) You need network continuity for ongoing treatment

If you're receiving care from a specific specialist team, or you have a procedure scheduled, network continuity stops being a convenience and becomes a medical safeguard. Marketplace networks can be narrower, and switching plans can mean switching doctors or redoing authorizations at exactly the wrong time.

COBRA can be valuable for continuity of care (network) and near-term simplicity. That "near-term" qualifier matters. COBRA can be the right move for a period of stability while you finish a treatment course, then you re-evaluate once the urgent medical phase passes.

3) You're in a tight enrollment window and COBRA buys you breathing room

As we saw, timing rules matter. You may have limited days to enroll in a Marketplace plan after losing employer coverage. COBRA paperwork can also have deadlines. When your life is in transition, "breathing room" is a real resource.

COBRA can function as a controlled pause: keep coverage uninterrupted while you do the Marketplace due diligence properly (networks, prescriptions, total cost). The goal is not to avoid shopping. The goal is to shop when you can think straight.

4) You value administrative simplicity and predictability in a year that's already chaotic

Some years you don't have bandwidth for an insurance learning curve. The plan you already know may reduce friction: fewer surprise denials, fewer "your doctor isn't in network" moments, fewer mysteries about how prescriptions are handled.

This is a legitimate reason, but it needs a price tag. Simplicity isn't free. COBRA is often what you pay for it.

The four reasons the Marketplace often wins (especially in the gap years)

If COBRA is continuity at full price, the Marketplace is often customization at subsidized price. That's why it's so frequently the long-run winner for gap-years planning.

1) Subsidies can turn an expensive year into a manageable year

If you qualify for premium tax credits, the Marketplace can be dramatically less expensive than COBRA on a monthly basis. COBRA premiums are generally the full cost; Marketplace premiums may be reduced depending on your situation. In gap-year planning, that subsidy is not a side benefit; it can be the core affordability engine.

This is where total-cost thinking matters. Lower premiums might be paired with higher deductibles, so you still need the calm/busy/bad year test. But if COBRA is costing $1,200/month and a Marketplace plan is $250/month after subsidies, you don't need an advanced spreadsheet to know which option deserves serious attention.

2) You get to choose a plan designed for your current life, not your old job

Employer plans are built for an employer's workforce and bargaining strategy. Your priorities may now be different: you might prioritize low worst-case exposure, a specific health system, or a particular prescription structure. The Marketplace lets you pick a plan that matches the new version of your life.

3) You can re-shop every year as prices and benchmarks move

Marketplace pricing shifts year-to-year, as we saw, and re-shopping is part of the game. COBRA is not a yearly optimization tool. It's a continuation mechanism. If you stay on COBRA long-term, you're usually paying a premium for the privilege of not deciding.

4) COBRA is expensive enough that "a little worse coverage" can still be a better deal

This is uncomfortable but often true. COBRA can keep you in a rich network with predictable rules, but the premium can be so high that even a less generous Marketplace plan ends up cheaper on an annual basis—including out-of-pocket costs—for many households.

The trick is to compare honestly: net premiums plus expected out-of-pocket spending, with the worst-case number staring you in the face. Don't let a low deductible seduce you into paying an absurd premium if you're unlikely to use much care.

Switching rules: the timing is not intuitive

Marketplace vs COBRA switching is timing-sensitive; consumers need the right enrollment window/opportunity to move from COBRA to Marketplace coverage. This is the part that creates real-world regret: people take COBRA "for now" and assume they can switch later whenever they get tired of the bill. That assumption can be wrong.

The practical implication isn't to memorize every rule. It's to plan the switch points before you commit:

- If you take COBRA, decide whether it's a short bridge to the next open enrollment or a longer-term choice.
- If you want the Marketplace, try to enroll at the first clean opportunity rather than assuming you'll have another one on demand.

As we saw, planning backward from coverage end dates is not optional. Insurance punishes improvisation.

Employer offers: the option that can quietly block subsidies

Now for the part that surprises people the first time it happens: you can do everything "right" on the Marketplace website and still discover at tax time that you weren't eligible for subsidies. The reason often traces back to employer coverage availability.

Premium Tax Credit (PTC) eligibility is generally blocked if a tax family member is eligible for an affordable employer-sponsored plan that provides minimum value (even if the person declines to enroll). That's a strong rule with strong consequences. It means that an employer offer can function like a gatekeeper: not just "another option," but a factor that determines whether Marketplace subsidies are on the table.

Two subtleties make this worth careful attention:

- *Eligibility matters, not enrollment.* Declining the employer plan doesn't restore subsidy eligibility if the offer was affordable and minimum value under the rules.
- *The offer can come from a spouse's employer.* This is where families get tripped up: one spouse retires, the other works. The working spouse's employer offer can affect the whole household's subsidy picture.

This is why "coverage paths first" is so powerful. You're not simply choosing between plans; you're choosing between systems with different rules.

Spouse coverage and the post-2022 "family glitch" fix

For years, families ran into a painful puzzle: an employer plan might be affordable for the employee alone but unaffordable to cover the whole family. Under older rules, that could block the spouse and dependents from Marketplace subsidies even when employer family coverage was wildly expensive.

The "family glitch" fix framework (effective for plan years after 2022) changes affordability determination for spouses/dependents, making it newly possible in some cases for family members to qualify for Marketplace subsidies when employer family coverage is unaffordable.

In human terms: it created a more realistic test for whether the family has access to reasonably priced employer coverage. That means spouse-and-kids planning deserves a fresh look each year, especially if employer premiums change.

The practical planning move is to treat employer coverage like a set of toggles you must evaluate, not a yes/no question:

- Is the employee-only coverage affordable?
- Is the family coverage affordable (under the post-2022 framework)?
- If family coverage is unaffordable, can the spouse/dependents use the Marketplace with subsidies while the employee stays on the employer plan?

This is one of the few areas where a small misunderstanding can cost thousands. It's also an area where the "cheap Marketplace plan" you see on the screen might be an illusion if the employer offer blocks subsidies.

A grounded way to compare paths: price, continuity, subsidy impact, hassle

A clean comparison doesn't require perfect precision. It requires that you measure the right things.

Price (annual, not monthly)

- COBRA: full premium (often up to 102% of plan cost) plus your expected out-of-pocket spending.

- Marketplace: net premium after subsidies (if eligible) plus expected out-of-pocket spending, plus your worst-case exposure comfort level.
- Employer/spouse plan: employee contribution plus cost-sharing, with the key add-on: what it does to subsidy eligibility for other household members.

Continuity

- Do you keep your doctors and hospitals?
- Do you keep your prescriptions on the same terms?
- Do you keep deductibles already satisfied?

Subsidy impact

The Marketplace is not merely another store. It's a store that may offer you a discount, but only if you meet eligibility rules. Employer offers can block that discount. If subsidies matter to your plan, you want to know early, not in April with a tax form.

Hassle

Hassle is real cost, just not in dollars. It's time on the phone, time coordinating referrals, time finding new doctors, and time fighting claims. COBRA often reduces hassle. Marketplace plans can be smooth, but switching always comes with some friction. If you're already dealing with a major life change, hassle might be the deciding factor.

Three real-world "bridge strategies" that work

Most households aren't choosing between pure COBRA for 18 months and pure Marketplace forever. They're stitching together coverage that matches what's happening medically and financially.

Bridge strategy 1: COBRA to finish a medical year, then Marketplace at the clean reset

This is common and often elegant:

- Take COBRA to preserve the deductible/out-of-pocket progress and provider continuity through December.
- Use open enrollment to choose a Marketplace plan for January 1, when everything resets anyway.

It aligns with the insurance calendar reality: switching is least painful at year boundaries.

Bridge strategy 2: Marketplace immediately, with aggressive network and drug verification

If subsidies make Marketplace coverage dramatically cheaper and you're not in the middle of complex care, moving right away can save substantial money. The key is doing the network and formulary reality checks so you don't buy cheap coverage that can't be used conveniently.

Bridge strategy 3: Split coverage within the household under the post-2022 family framework

In some households, the cleanest move is:

- Employee stays on an employer plan.

- Spouse and/or dependents use the Marketplace with subsidies if employer family coverage is unaffordable under the current rules.

This is not a "hack." It's a legitimate outcome under the updated affordability approach. The household wins by not overpaying for employer family coverage that doesn't price sensibly.

A final sanity check before you pick a path

Right before committing, ask a question that's almost embarrassingly practical:

> If I choose this path, what do I most want to *not think about* for the next 90 days?

If the answer is "my upcoming surgery" or "keeping my specialist" or "not switching prescriptions," COBRA may be worth the premium for a period. If the answer is "writing big checks every month," the Marketplace likely deserves a hard look. If the answer is "not triggering a subsidy mess," then the employer-offer analysis needs to be clean and conservative.

The best bridge coverage is the one that fits the situation you actually have: your medical calendar, your budget tolerance for worst-case exposure, and the rules that govern subsidy eligibility. The moment you see those as separate axes—cost, continuity, subsidy access, and hassle—the choice becomes less emotional and more strategic.

Chapter 5

Running the Plan Year by Year

Early retirement health coverage is not something you set once and forget, like a toaster warranty. It behaves more like tending a garden: income shifts, plan prices move, provider networks change, and a small update at the right time can prevent a costly mess later. This chapter shows readers how to run their ACA strategy year by year with a calm, repeatable routine that keeps premiums, subsidies, and coverage aligned with real life.

5.1 Forecasting MAGI with Guardrails and Scenarios

A Marketplace income estimate has a weird job. It's asked to be both a prediction and a steering wheel. Predict too low and you may get more upfront subsidy than you ultimately qualify for. Predict too high and you pay more each month than you needed to, essentially lending money to the government interest-free until you file your return. Either way, the final answer is taken from your tax return, not your hopes and intentions.

So the goal isn't a single "correct" number. The goal is to design a year that can absorb surprises without wrecking your health-insurance pricing. Think in ranges, not point estimates. Think guardrails, not tightropes.

Start with a boring truth: the plan year will not be boring

Early retirees often have the most *interesting* income. Not necessarily high income—just income that shows up in chunks, drifts upward without asking permission, and occasionally explodes because markets and life do what they do. A traditional paycheck is predictable: same cadence, same withholding, same W-2. Gap-year income is the opposite:

- A Roth conversion that feels like a bookkeeping entry, until you remember it's counted as income.
- A brokerage account that throws off dividends and capital gains distributions on a schedule you don't control.
- A surprise consulting project that seems "small," because you're thinking in *monthly* terms, and the Marketplace cares about the *year*.
- An inheritance, a property sale, an employer payout, a K-1 that arrives late and refuses to be neat.

If you're trying to forecast MAGI precisely with those ingredients, you'll spend the year either anxious or wrong. Better to build three versions of the year and manage toward the one that keeps you safely inside your chosen subsidy zone.

The three-year method: base, optimistic, pessimistic

The trick is to stop asking, "What will MAGI be?" and instead ask, "What are three believable ways this year could go?" Give each version a personality:

- *Base year*: the most likely year if nothing weird happens.
- *Optimistic year*: markets behave, opportunities show up, maybe you do a little work, maybe a planned gain becomes attractive.

- *Pessimistic year*: something disappoints—less work, lower distributions, an investment loss you can't fully use this year, or you deliberately pull back on income to stay comfortable.

It sounds almost too simple, but it changes how you make decisions in June. With a single forecast, every new 1099 feels like an ambush. With scenarios, it's just information: "Ah. We're drifting from base toward optimistic. Time to switch tactics."

Build the forecast the way a mechanic listens for a rattle

You don't start by guessing the whole engine. You start with the parts you can hear.

Step 1: Write down the stable floor

These are the items that tend to arrive on schedule and can usually be estimated within a tight band:

- Social Security (if any) and the portion that ends up in your Marketplace MAGI calculation.
- Pension income.
- Annuity payments.
- Required minimum distributions (if they apply to you).
- Bond interest in taxable accounts (fairly predictable).
- Any ongoing part-time job with regular hours.

This stable floor is comforting—and dangerous—because it can lull you into thinking you're done. You're not done until you've chased down the "quiet increasers."

Step 2: Add the quiet increasers (the stuff that creeps)

Quiet increasers are small on any one statement, but excellent at turning December into a surprise.

Common culprits:

- *Ordinary dividends*: you might have a decent estimate, but they still drift when markets move or funds adjust payouts.
- *Capital gain distributions* from mutual funds: you may not control timing, and they can be larger than you expect in strong markets (or when a fund has internal turnover).
- *Interest on cash and CDs*: rates reset, balances change, and "safe" money can generate surprisingly meaningful income when yields are higher.
- *Tax-exempt interest*: it doesn't show up in AGI, but it does show up in ACA MAGI. That muni bond fund can be a stealth contributor.

None of these are a moral failing. They're just the difference between "I spent $70,000 this year" and "my MAGI was $70,000." Cash flow is chatty; MAGI is particular.

Step 3: List the lumpy levers (the stuff you can choose)

These are the items that tend to arrive in chunks and are often partially under your control:

- *Roth conversions*: the cleanest income lever and the easiest one to overshoot if you "just do it all at once."
- *Realized capital gains*: selling appreciated shares, trimming a concentrated position, harvesting gains for basis management.
- *Self-employment or consulting income*: sometimes controllable by how much work you accept and when invoices are paid.

- *Rental income*: especially variable if there's a vacancy, a major repair, or depreciation changes.
- *One-time events*: severance, retention bonuses, relocation reimbursements, settlement income, a business sale.

These levers are where you create your guardrails. They're also where people get into trouble—because a lever that can increase income can also increase it *fast*.

Guardrails: the safety margin that keeps you from paying for one "oops"

Guardrails are simply a buffer between your working plan and the edge of a pricing change you'd hate.

The edge could be:

- A subsidy drop that makes your monthly bill jump more than you're comfortable with.
- Losing access to cost-sharing reductions (if you're in that income neighborhood) and watching deductibles and copays balloon.
- A repayment surprise at tax time because too much help was paid on your behalf during the year.

A useful guardrail has two properties:

1. It's big enough to cover your most likely forecasting errors.
2. It's small enough that you're not voluntarily overpaying all year for no reason.

The size depends on your income ingredients. If your income is mostly pension plus a small IRA distribution, a tight buffer might be fine. If you own mutual funds that like to distribute gains in December and you're doing Roth conversions, you need a wider shoulder on the road.

A practical way to choose a buffer

Instead of arguing with yourself about the "right" number, rate each volatile source as:

- *Low drift*: likely within a few hundred dollars of estimate.
- *Medium drift*: could easily be off by a couple thousand.
- *High drift*: could be off by $5,000, $10,000, or more without trying.

Then size your buffer to cover one "high drift" surprise plus one "medium drift" surprise. That's not scientific. It's realistic.

Example: if capital gain distributions could be $0 or $6,000, and side income could end up $3,000 higher than expected, planning a $10,000 guardrail below your upper comfort threshold is not cautious—it's simply acknowledging how these numbers behave in the wild.

A simple three-scenario table (you can do it on paper)

You don't need fancy software. You need a page that forces you to separate what's stable from what's optional.

Here's a template you can copy into a spreadsheet or notebook. The point isn't the formatting; it's the thinking.

Income item (counts toward ACA MAGI)	*Pessimistic*	*Base*	*Optimistic*
Stable floor (pension, Social Security portion, etc.)			
Dividends (ordinary + qualified)			
Interest (taxable + tax-exempt add-back)			
Capital gain distributions (funds/ETFs)			
Net capital gains from sales you control			
Roth conversions (your dial)			
Part-time / consulting income			
Rental / business income			
Other (one-time items)			
Estimated ACA MAGI			

Two notes make this tool actually work:

- Put your *choices* (Roth conversions, gain realization, extra work) on their own lines. Otherwise, you'll "accidentally" bake a choice into your forecast and forget it was optional.
- Write the optimistic scenario as something you'd be *happy* about. If your optimistic scenario is actually "the year goes wrong and I'm forced into a bad choice," that's not optimistic—that's a risk plan, and it belongs in a different box.

Why the volatile items are so sneaky

Some income sources feel like they shouldn't matter because they don't feel like spending power. Others feel like they shouldn't count because no cash changes hands. The Marketplace doesn't care about your feelings. It cares about what ends up in the MAGI calculation on your return.

Here's how four common culprits quietly shove the year around.

Capital gains: the "I sold something" tax you forget you chose

Capital gains aren't a monthly paycheck. They're a decision. That's why they're dangerous: you can make them appear with a click.

Common patterns that cause drift:

- *Portfolio cleanup*: selling a long-held position to simplify or reduce risk.
- *Rebalancing*: trimming winners after a strong run.
- *"Just taking some profits"*: the most expensive casual phrase in early retirement.

The guardrail move: treat large sales like a two-step process. First, estimate the gain. Second, decide whether the gain belongs in this calendar year or next. If the gain pushes your optimistic scenario into "regret territory," you either sell less, donate appreciated shares (if charitable giving fits), or delay the sale.

Also remember that gains are *net*: gains minus losses. Losses can help, but they don't give you unlimited room. Large losses can be useful, but they don't create a blank check for conversions and gains in the same year without consequences elsewhere.

Dividends: the drip that fills the bucket

Dividends feel passive and small. Then you add them up.

Two dividend surprises show up in real life:

- *Market surprise*: a strong year increases payouts, especially if you hold dividend-heavy funds.
- *Holding surprise*: you may not realize how dividend-rich your portfolio has become after years of "income" investing.

The guardrail move: use last year's 1099 as a starting point, then add a cushion if markets are up materially or if you changed holdings. If you hold mutual funds, assume you may also get year-end capital gain distributions that don't care about your planning.

Roth conversions: the clean lever that can punch through your ceiling

A Roth conversion is one of the most powerful tools in the gap years—and it's also the easiest way to blow past your target. Why? Because it feels like moving money from one pocket to another. No lifestyle change. No spending spree. Just an accounting move.

But a conversion is income. Full stop.

The guardrail move: convert in installments, not as a one-and-done annual event.

A practical rhythm that many early retirees like is:

- Wait until you have at least some visibility into dividends, interest, and any part-time income.
- Convert in chunks during the year (monthly or quarterly), leaving room for late-year surprises.
- Keep a "do not cross" number for your year-to-date MAGI estimate, not just for your final goal.

This is less about math and more about behavior. A conversion plan that requires perfect December discipline is a plan that will occasionally fail in December.

Part-time work: the income you deserve, arriving exactly when you forgot to plan for it

Many early retirees underestimate how psychologically easy it is to say yes to "just a little work." The work itself can be great. The problem is that it often arrives mid-year, after you've already set your health plan, started a conversion schedule, or realized some gains.

The guardrail move: treat part-time income like a first-class citizen in the forecast. Don't stick it into "other." Give it a line item with a range.

Also, be mindful of timing. A check received in December is still this year's income. If you can legitimately shift invoice timing without playing games, that can be the difference between a calm tax season and a nasty surprise.

Your best friend: a "decision budget" for optional income

Once you've built the stable floor and estimated the creepers, you can create something that feels oddly freeing: a decision budget.

Decision budget = (upper comfort limit for the year) – (stable floor) – (reasonable estimate of quiet increasers)

What's left is the amount of income you can "spend" on optional moves: conversions, gains, extra work, maybe pulling money from a pre-tax account instead of a brokerage account.

Two important uses:

- *It turns trade-offs into choices.* "If I do a $15,000 conversion, I probably won't realize that $12,000 gain this year."
- *It prevents double-spending your headroom.* Without a decision budget, it's easy to separately approve three "small" moves that add up to a big overshoot.

Make the decision budget different for each scenario. In the optimistic year, you may have less headroom because dividends and gains are higher. That's fine. That's reality.

The "take less upfront help" lever (a sanity tool, not a math flex)

There's an underused way to make forecasting mistakes less painful: you can choose to take less advance subsidy than you appear eligible for based on your estimate.

This is not about depriving yourself. It's about buying optionality.

If your income is hard to forecast—because you're doing conversions, consulting, or managing a taxable portfolio—a smaller upfront subsidy can reduce the chance that a good year turns into an April repayment story. You're essentially choosing a smaller discount now in exchange for fewer sharp edges later.

This lever pairs well with guardrails:

- Guardrails reduce the odds of an overshoot.
- Taking less upfront help reduces the sting if an overshoot happens anyway.

Some people love this approach because it makes the whole system feel less like a trap. Others prefer to take the full amount monthly and manage tightly. The right answer is the one that lets you sleep and still execute your broader plan.

Mid-year monitoring without making it your hobby

Forecasting is not a one-time ritual. It's a light check-in habit—like glancing at the weather before you drive.

A simple cadence that works for many households:

- *Quarterly check*: update year-to-date dividends, interest, and realized gains. Re-estimate the full-year number.
- *Trigger check*: any time you do something that creates income on purpose (a conversion, a big sale, a contract), update the forecast within a week while the decision is still fresh.

- *Late-summer check*: this is the big one. By late summer you often have enough data to decide whether to accelerate conversions, harvest gains, or back off.

The key is to monitor the *drivers*, not just the total. If dividends are running hot, you don't want to learn that in January. You want to learn it while you still have levers left.

Common forecasting traps (and the simple fix for each)

These are the mistakes that create most of the "How did we end up here?" stories.

Trap: confusing withdrawals with income

Spending from savings feels like income because it pays the bills. But only certain withdrawals create MAGI. The fix is to keep your cash-flow plan and your MAGI forecast on separate pages. Let them talk to each other, but don't marry them.

Trap: doing one big income move early in the year

A large conversion in January feels productive. It's also done with the least information you'll have all year. The fix is to split big moves into tranches, especially if other income sources are variable.

Trap: forgetting the add-backs

Most early retirees remember the big pieces—IRA distributions, conversions, realized gains. The fix is to explicitly list the MAGI add-backs you personally have exposure to (tax-exempt interest is the big one for many households). If you don't have any, great—write "none expected" so you don't have to wonder later.

Trap: treating "optimistic" as "unlikely"

Optimistic doesn't mean fantasy. It means, "A year that would feel good." Markets up is not fantasy; it's Tuesday. Getting offered a small consulting gig is not fantasy; it's what happens when smart people retire and other smart people notice.

The fix is to write an optimistic scenario that you would not be shocked to live through. If that optimistic number would force you into an outcome you hate, your guardrails are too thin or your plan relies too heavily on income you don't control.

A realistic example: how a calm plan turns chaotic

Imagine a household with a clean base plan:

- Stable floor: $38,000 (pension and a small taxable IRA distribution)
- Expected dividends/interest: $6,000
- Planned Roth conversion: $20,000
- Total base estimate: $64,000

So far, so tidy. Now add three normal events:

- Mutual fund capital gain distributions arrive: $4,500 (not planned)
- A friend refers a short consulting gig: $7,000 (fun, manageable)
- A portfolio cleanup sale realizes gains: $6,000 (felt like housekeeping)

That's $17,500 of additional income without anyone "messing up." The household that thought they were living at $64,000 ends up near $81,500—before any late-year adjustments.

A three-scenario forecast would have forced those items onto the page as possibilities. Guardrails would have reserved space for them. And the decision budget would have made it obvious that the $20,000 conversion wasn't automatically compatible with every other good idea that showed up.

Tactical playbook: what to do when you're drifting upward

Sometimes you'll see the optimistic scenario becoming real. That's not failure. That's information.

Here are clean, non-panicky moves that can bring the year back inside your chosen comfort zone:

- *Pause or reduce Roth conversions* for the remainder of the year.
- *Delay discretionary realized gains* (sell fewer shares, or postpone a cleanup sale).
- *Shift charitable giving to appreciated shares* (if you were already planning to give).
- *Watch invoice timing* for legitimate flexibility in self-employment cash receipts.
- *Consider taking less advance subsidy going forward* if you're worried about the year-end reconciliation outcome.

Notice what's not on that list: "Panic and change your life." Most of the time, you don't need drama. You need a dial, and you need to turn it before December makes the decision for you.

The calm endgame: design a year that forgives you

A good MAGI forecast doesn't prove you're smart. It makes it hard for one random event to make you feel stupid.

Three scenarios keep you from anchoring on a single fragile number. Guardrails keep small surprises from becoming big consequences.

And a decision budget keeps you from double-counting headroom like it's an unlimited resource.

The result is a plan that behaves like a good piece of equipment: not delicate, not mysterious, and not offended by real life.

5.2 Updating the Marketplace When Life Changes

The Marketplace isn't a set-it-and-forget-it product. It behaves more like a thermostat: you set it based on what you think the year will feel like, and then life walks over and opens a window. If you never touch the controls again, the room still has heat—but you shouldn't be surprised if the bill looks odd later.

The good news is that reporting changes is usually less dramatic than people imagine. You're not "confessing" anything. You're aligning a moving estimate with a moving reality so the math doesn't ambush you at tax time.

Why timing matters: the subsidy you get now is an advance on a future calculation

Money that reduces your monthly premium during the year is based on what you told the Marketplace you expected to earn. Your tax return later decides what you actually qualified for. That gap—between estimate and final—gets reconciled.

If you report a change promptly, the Marketplace can adjust the advance assistance so it's closer to what you'll truly qualify for by year-end. That's the whole point: fewer months running "too rich" or "too lean."

One practical wrinkle makes procrastination costly: reported changes lead to a redetermination notice and are implemented prospectively—often with a future effective date. In plain English, the system usually can't go back in time and "fix" last month. So waiting doesn't keep things stable; it simply locks in more months of mismatch.

The psychological hurdle: it feels like bureaucracy, but it's really maintenance

Most early retirees don't mind optimizing a withdrawal plan or rebalancing a portfolio. Yet a Marketplace update can trigger a special kind of dread: logins, passwords, notices, and the fear of accidentally breaking coverage.

A useful mindset shift: treat your Marketplace account the way you treat autopay. You don't "set it up once and never look again." You check it after a move, after a bank change, after a card replacement—because small maintenance prevents big interruptions.

HealthCare.gov's action path is straightforward: log in and use "Report a Life Change" to update income, household, address, offers of coverage, and other application items. If the website makes you want to throw your laptop, the Marketplace Call Center can help. That's not an emergency resource reserved for disasters; it's there for normal humans with normal questions.

Noise versus signal: not every wiggle deserves an update

A mid-year plan doesn't need to react to every tiny fluctuation. If your interest income is running $40 ahead of schedule, that's not a life change; that's Tuesday.

The updates worth making are the ones that reliably move the big levers:

- household size or who's on the tax return,
- geography (address changes can change plans and networks),
- eligibility for other coverage (especially an offer of employer coverage),

- income changes large enough to materially alter the assistance amount you're receiving each month.

A useful test: *Would I care about this change if it lasted the entire year?* If the answer is yes, update. If it's a one-off blip that reverses next month, you may be better served by tightening your own guardrails (like taking less advance help) rather than whipping the application around.

Income changes: the most common update, and the easiest to mishandle

Income changes are tricky because they come in two flavors: predictable and sneaky.

Predictable changes tend to be easier emotionally:

- a spouse returns to work,
- a pension begins,
- a planned Roth conversion schedule ramps up,
- a consulting contract starts with known terms.

Sneaky changes are the ones that feel small until they aren't:

- a string of "just a little" freelance checks,
- an unexpectedly large year-end fund distribution,
- a gain realized because you cleaned up a holding at the wrong moment,
- a side business that has a very good quarter.

The mishandling usually looks like this: you treat the advance assistance like a coupon you either "deserve" or "don't deserve," and you avoid updating because you don't want the coupon to shrink. That's understandable—and it's also how people walk into repayment surprises. IRS Pub 974 is blunt about the practical consequence: reporting changes promptly allows the Marketplace to adjust the advance assistance to better match what you'll qualify for at year-end.

A more calming approach is to view the monthly discount as provisional. If your income rises, the discount should shrink. That's not punishment; it's the system doing what you asked it to do: track your best estimate.

How big is "big enough" to report?

There's no one dollar amount that fits every household, because the sensitivity depends on where you are relative to subsidy thresholds and how much help you're receiving.

Instead, anchor on impact:

- If the change would move your annual MAGI estimate by thousands (not hundreds), it's usually worth updating.
- If you're near a threshold you care about (for example, you're intentionally staying in a particular band), smaller changes can matter more.
- If the change is durable—"this is our new normal for the rest of the year"—update sooner rather than later.

The goal isn't perfection. The goal is to avoid being wrong in the same direction for ten months.

Household changes: the update people delay because it feels personal

Household changes can feel awkward to report because they're emotional events: marriage, divorce, a dependent moving in or moving out, a birth, a death. But the Marketplace doesn't experience your life event; it experiences math.

These updates matter because the Marketplace is built around who is expected to be on the tax return—your "tax household." Health-

Care.gov specifically flags changes in tax filing status as reportable. That's the system telling you, politely, "This changes the entire calculation."

A few real-life situations that deserve prompt attention:

Marriage

Marriage can be financially wonderful and administratively annoying. Two incomes and one tax return can swing eligibility dramatically. If one spouse had coverage and the other didn't, or if one spouse has work income that changes the household's annual estimate, waiting can create months of misaligned assistance.

Also watch the subtle version: you get married late in the year and assume it "mostly counts next year." For taxes and the Marketplace, that assumption can be expensive.

Divorce or separation

A separation can change filing status, household size, and address—sometimes all at once. That's exactly the kind of compound change that can break things if you don't update. The goal is not to sort out the entire emotional situation inside a web form. The goal is to stop running the wrong household through the subsidy engine.

A dependent arrives (or stops being your dependent)

A dependent moving in—an adult child in a tough job market, a grandchild, an elderly parent—can change household size for eligibility purposes, but only if they're expected to be part of the tax household. The Marketplace application is asking a tax question, not a living-room question. If the tax return will include them, the update can shift the assistance calculation.

The reverse is also common: a child graduates, starts work, and is no longer a dependent. Many households keep running the old setup out of habit, then wonder why the numbers don't reconcile cleanly.

Address moves: the change that looks harmless until your network disappears

Moving is the most underestimated Marketplace update. People think, "Same state, same insurer, we'll keep the plan." Then they discover the Marketplace is county-based in ways that feel almost medieval.

An address change can alter:

- which plans are available at all,
- provider networks (your "in-network" doctor might instantly become out-of-network),
- premiums and the benchmark used in the subsidy calculation,
- drug formularies and preferred pharmacies.

This isn't about being dramatic; it's about avoiding an unpleasant surprise at the pharmacy counter.

If you move, update the address promptly. Not next open enrollment. Not "after we unpack." Promptly. The reason is practical: you may be enrolled in a plan that is no longer offered in your new area, or you may have access to different options that better match your new geography.

Other coverage eligibility: the update that can flip the whole story

Certain coverage changes are so important that delaying them can create more than a tax mess; they can create eligibility confusion and administrative headaches.

HealthCare.gov explicitly includes offers of coverage among the items you can update using "Report a Life Change." Take that seriously. A new offer of employer coverage for you or a spouse can change whether Marketplace assistance is available or how the Marketplace views your options.

This is especially relevant for early retirees whose spouse keeps working, returns to work, or picks up a job with benefits mid-year. The family may still prefer a Marketplace plan for network reasons, but eligibility and assistance calculations can be affected by the existence of other coverage options. The key is not to guess—update the application with what changed so the system can properly assess the household.

A timeline example: why "I'll update later" quietly costs real money

Consider a household that estimated $60,000 of annual MAGI. In May, a spouse returns to work and the household now expects $78,000.

If they update quickly:

- the Marketplace recalculates,
- a redetermination notice arrives,
- the monthly discount adjusts prospectively (often starting in a future month).

If they wait until November:

- they receive the old, larger monthly discount for many additional months,
- the prospective adjustment arrives late (so it doesn't offset much),
- the reconciliation at tax time has to clean up a much larger mismatch.

The frustrating part is that waiting often *feels* like it avoids pain—until the pain arrives in a lump sum. Prompt updating is boring. Boring is good.

How to make updates less painful: keep a "Marketplace packet"

The main reason people postpone updates is not ideology; it's friction. You can reduce friction by keeping a small set of numbers and documents handy so updates become a 15-minute task instead of an afternoon.

A simple "Marketplace packet" can be:

- your current annual MAGI estimate (base case) and your guardrail buffer,
- year-to-date income totals for the main categories you monitor,
- your most recent pay stub or benefit letter if a new income stream began,
- the basic details of any coverage offer (who is covered, when it starts).

You don't need to hoard paperwork. You just want to avoid the common trap of abandoning the update halfway through because you can't find a number.

What happens after you report: fewer surprises if you expect the paperwork

After you submit an update, it's normal to receive a redetermination notice. That's not a sign you did something wrong; it's the system documenting the new eligibility result.

Also expect the new numbers to take effect prospectively. That "prospective" word is a big deal. It's why prompt reporting matters, and it's why "I'll fix it at tax time" is a strategy with sharp edges:

tax time can reconcile dollars, but it can't retroactively make your monthly cash flow comfortable.

A short list of changes that are usually not worth a mid-year scramble

Some things are real but often don't deserve immediate action unless they're large or persistent:

- a small swing in bank interest,
- a one-time dividend that doesn't meaningfully alter your annual estimate,
- a minor change in expected deductions (the Marketplace is focused on income inputs; your tax return will ultimately settle the score).

If you're unsure, the deciding factor is usually magnitude and persistence. Small and temporary? Probably not. Large or durable? Yes.

A few "high drama" situations where a call is worth it

Some updates are emotionally draining or logistically complex. These are good candidates for the Marketplace Call Center, not because you can't do them online, but because you deserve the support:

- a move combined with a household change,
- a divorce in progress with uncertain filing status,
- conflicting start dates for different coverage options,
- confusion about whether an offer of coverage needs to be reflected and how.

Calling doesn't make the policy questions vanish, but it can keep a simple update from becoming an error that takes hours to unwind.

The practical payoff: clean monthly pricing and a calmer tax season

A Marketplace plan is priced monthly, but judged annually. Updating life changes is how you keep those two clocks from drifting too far apart.

Do it promptly for the high-impact changes—income that truly shifted, a household that truly changed, an address that truly moved, a new coverage option that truly exists. Ignore the small noise. Expect a redetermination notice. Expect prospective implementation. And remember the core idea: you're not trying to produce a perfect prediction. You're trying to keep the year from becoming a long series of avoidable mismatches.

5.3 Annual Re-Enrollments and Smart Re-Shopping

Auto-renewal is a little like your streaming service quietly rolling into the next month: convenient, frictionless, and oddly confident that nothing about your preferences has changed. Health insurance doesn't deserve that kind of trust. The Marketplace can automatically re-enroll you if you don't act by the open enrollment deadlines, and you can still switch through the end of open enrollment—but "still switch later" is cold comfort if you realize in January that your doctor is gone or your cheapest prescription is suddenly full price.

The underlying reason is simple: the plan you bought last year is not a product sitting on a shelf waiting for you. It's a contract in a living ecosystem—insurers adjust pricing, counties redraw what's available, networks reshuffle, and the subsidy math is pegged to a moving benchmark. Treating open enrollment like a fresh buying decision isn't being fussy. It's basic risk management.

The annual reset you can't see: redetermination, benchmark drift, and quiet recalculations

The Marketplace doesn't just renew *your* plan. It re-runs eligibility and financial help for the coming year through an annual redetermination process (45 CFR 155.335 is the regulatory backbone for how that happens). And on the federal platform, CMS guidance explains that Marketplaces can request updated IRS data for enrollees receiving APTC/CSR who authorized data pulls. Translation: your file can get refreshed whether or not you touch it. That's helpful, but it's not mind-reading. If your household changed, your income pattern shifted, or you intentionally manage MAGI tightly, it's worth verifying that the numbers being used match the reality you're planning.

Then there's the benchmark: the second-lowest-cost Silver plan in your area, which acts like the reference price for how subsidies are calculated. If *your* plan's premium barely changes but the benchmark moves a lot, the monthly discount can change anyway. People experience this as "my plan didn't change, but my cost did," which is infuriating until you realize the benchmark is a separate object.

Open enrollment is where you get to respond intentionally to all those moving parts instead of living with whatever the system assumed.

Why last year's winner can lose next year

A good plan choice is never purely *low premium* or *low deductible*. It's a match between your expected usage, your risk tolerance, and the local market's quirks. Those quirks change.

Here are the repeat offenders—the reasons a previously excellent plan becomes a bad deal without doing anything "wrong."

Benchmark changes: your discount is anchored to a plan you may not even like

Because the discount is tied to the benchmark, the *relative* pricing among plans matters as much as the sticker price of your current plan.

If the benchmark gets cheaper, subsidies can shrink, and many plans become more expensive after assistance. If the benchmark gets more expensive, subsidies can grow, sometimes making higher-metal plans look oddly attractive. Either way, ignoring the benchmark is like ignoring the tide because your boat is the same boat.

A practical habit: every year, identify the benchmark plan's premium for your household and treat it as a "market index" for your area. You don't have to buy it. You just want to know what the subsidy engine is using as its ruler.

Silver loading: the pricing quirk that can flip the best deal upside down

Silver loading is one of those industry phrases that sounds like a shipping problem. What it really means is that in many places, insurers price certain extra costs into Silver plan premiums. The result can be bizarre: Gold plans sometimes end up priced close to Silver plans, and Bronze plans sometimes look cheaper than you'd expect relative to the subsidy math.

You don't need to become a policy wonk to benefit from this. You just need to accept one truth: *metal levels don't price in a neat ladder.* Some years, the value is sitting in a surprising corner of the menu.

Network shifts: the plan can keep its name and still drop your doctor

Provider networks are living organisms. Hospitals renegotiate. physician groups change affiliations. insurers narrow networks to control costs. Some changes are announced clearly; others are effectively discovered at the worst possible moment: after the appointment, when the claim is denied.

Even if you rarely use care, networks matter. A "rarely" year can become a "suddenly" year, and the whole point of insurance is to be ready for the year you didn't schedule.

The sharp-edged reality: an auto-renewed plan can keep you insured while quietly changing which care is affordable.

Drug formularies: the pharmacy can turn into a price trap overnight

A formulary is the plan's list of covered drugs and their tiers. Tiers drive copays and coinsurance; prior authorization rules drive hassle and delays.

Formulary changes don't just affect people with complex conditions. They can hit anyone who takes a single brand-name medication that lacks a good generic alternative—or anyone who discovers that a medication moved from a predictable copay to coinsurance subject to the deductible.

A disciplined routine is boring and powerful:

- Check each medication you actually take.
- Check the tier and whether the deductible applies.
- Check whether your preferred pharmacy is still "preferred."

That last one sounds petty until you're standing at the counter learning that your monthly cost doubled because you used the wrong chain.

Plan design changes: the premium stayed stable, but the out-of-pocket rules didn't

Plans can tweak copays, coinsurance, deductibles, and out-of-pocket maximums. The changes can be subtle enough to miss in a renewal notice and large enough to matter if you have a medium-to-high usage year.

One especially sneaky change is the trade:

- Lower premium, higher deductible.
- Same premium, higher specialist coinsurance.
- Similar deductible, worse prescription structure.

None of those are inherently bad. They're only bad if you sleepwalk into them.

Compare plans like a retiree, not like a coupon clipper

A monthly premium is emotionally loud because it hits your checking account twelve times a year. Out-of-pocket spending is emotionally quiet because it's uncertain—until it isn't.

A plan comparison that respects real life uses three usage levels:

- *Low use*: mostly preventive care, maybe a visit or two.
- *Medium use*: a couple of specialists, imaging, some ongoing prescriptions.
- *High use*: the year that includes surgery, an ER visit, an infusion drug, or a new diagnosis.

The goal isn't to predict which year you'll have. It's to know the financial story in each lane:

- What do I pay if nothing happens?
- What do I pay if something manageable happens?
- What do I pay if life decides to get dramatic?

At a minimum, every plan can be reduced to three numbers you can hold in your head:

- annual premium you expect to pay after assistance,
- expected out-of-pocket in a typical year for your situation,
- worst-case exposure (premium plus the plan's out-of-pocket maximum for covered, in-network care).

That third number is the one that keeps early retirement from feeling fragile. It's the "how bad can this get?" number.

A repeatable method that doesn't require an actuarial degree

A smart comparison doesn't mean reading every PDF. It means pulling the few levers that actually change the outcome.

1) Start with your non-negotiables

Before you look at premiums, decide what would make a plan unusable:

- one or two must-have doctors or hospitals,
- a must-have medication (or a class of medications),
- a travel pattern that makes certain networks unrealistic,
- HSA compatibility, if that's part of your strategy.

This step prevents the classic mistake: falling in love with a price on a plan you can't comfortably use.

2) Read the renewal notice like it's a contract amendment (because it is)

Renewal materials are not marketing; they're disclosures. You're hunting for changes:

- premium change for the coming year,
- deductible and out-of-pocket maximum,
- changes to copays/coinsurance for the services you actually use,
- network and formulary notices.

If you only do one thing, do this: check whether the plan is still offered in your area and whether your key providers remain in-network.

3) Use a three-lane cost comparison

For each plan you're considering, write down:

- annual premium (after any assistance you expect based on your current forecast),
- expected out-of-pocket for low/medium/high usage,
- worst-case exposure (premium plus out-of-pocket max).

That middle number—expected out-of-pocket—doesn't need to be perfect. It needs to be honest. If you take two brand-name prescriptions and see specialists, don't benchmark yourself as "low use" because you *feel* healthy.

4) Give extra skepticism to "cheap"

Cheap can be real value, or it can be a trap hiding in a deductible or a narrow network. The Marketplace is full of plans that are inexpensive precisely because they've designed the friction into the fine print.

A good rule: if a plan is dramatically cheaper than the nearby alternatives, ask *what it's refusing to pay for*:

- Is the network narrower?
- Does the deductible apply to more services?
- Are specialist visits coinsurance instead of copay?
- Are common drugs non-preferred?

None of those are automatically deal-breakers. They're simply the "price tag" you need to see.

A story that happens every year: the auto-renewal that keeps coverage but breaks the plan

A household chooses a Silver plan that fits their doctors and keeps their expected costs sane. The next year, they let auto-renewal ride because the premium change looks small.

January arrives. The plan is active. Coverage is continuous. So far, so good.

February arrives, and their specialist group has left the network. Not all doctors—just the ones they use. Suddenly "same plan" behaves like "new plan," except they didn't get the chance to choose it on purpose. They can still switch during open enrollment (if it's still open), but after that window closes, the household is stuck: insured, but effectively priced out of their established care.

Auto-renewal did what it promised: no lapse in coverage. It didn't promise that the plan still fits your life.

Calendar reality: effective dates reward the early shopper

CMS publishes official open enrollment windows and effective-date cutoffs for the federal Marketplace (state-based Marketplaces can vary). The practical takeaway is blunt: earlier action tends to preserve more options—more time to compare, more time to fix an application glitch, more time to make a deliberate selection that starts on January 1 rather than later.

If you wait until the last week, you're forcing a high-stakes purchase into the same mental space as holiday travel planning and end-of-year family chaos. That's not just unpleasant; it's how people end up keeping a plan by inertia.

A disciplined action checklist (fast, not fussy)

Open enrollment goes smoothly when you treat it like a short, scripted project with a clear "done" state.

Task	*What you're looking for*
Confirm household + income estimate	The application reflects your current reality; income aligns with your forecast guardrails.
Check auto-renewal status	Whether the system will re-enroll you if you do nothing (useful as a backstop, not a plan).
Read renewal changes	Premium, deductible, out-of-pocket max, and any service cost changes that affect you.
Verify doctors and facilities	Key providers are in-network for the coming year (not "were in-network last year").
Verify medications	Each medication's tier, deductible rules, and any prior authorization or step therapy flags.
Compare total annual cost in three lanes	Low/medium/high usage totals, plus worst-case exposure for peace of mind.
Sanity-check the "too cheap" option	If it's far cheaper, identify the trade-off (network, deductible scope, drug coverage).
Save proof	Download or save the plan summary and your final enrollment confirmation.

If this feels like more work than it should be, that's because it is. Health insurance shopping is not elegant. The win is that the work is concentrated into a predictable season, and it pays you back all year—sometimes in smaller monthly bills, sometimes in a network that doesn't betray you, and sometimes in the quiet knowledge that your worst-case number is one you can live with.

5.4 Building a Repeatable Operating Checklist

The biggest hidden cost in managing Marketplace coverage isn't the premium. It's the mental tab you keep open all year: *Did I estimate right? Did I forget to report something? What happens if we sell shares? Is our plan still the plan?* An open tab drains attention the same way a slow leak drains a tire—quietly, constantly, and usually noticed only when something feels off.

A repeatable checklist closes the tab. Not because it makes the system simple, but because it makes your responsibilities predictable. You stop relying on memory and motivation, and you start relying on a rhythm.

The core idea: build a calendar that tells you what to care about, and when

Marketplace planning has two clocks. One clock is the coverage calendar: enroll, pay, use care. The other is the tax calendar: reconcile the help you received with the income you actually had. The stress comes from letting those clocks drift apart.

A good operating checklist acts like a bridge between them. It creates a handful of recurring moments where you deliberately look at your income estimate, your plan details, and your paperwork. Not daily. Not obsessively. Just often enough that "surprises" become boring adjustments.

If you only remember one principle, make it this one: *do the administrative work while you still have choices*. That means before open enrollment closes, before December income becomes unchangeable, and before tax deadlines turn a missing form into a crisis.

Your annual workflow in four seasons (plus one rule that prevents headaches)

Think of the year as four short projects, each with a clear finish line. The goal isn't to become an insurance hobbyist; it's to avoid last-minute scrambles.

Season 1: Early-year setup (January–February)

January has an odd emotional quality: it feels like a fresh start, but it's also when your plan is brand new and your memory of open enrollment is already fading. This is the moment to put your choices on rails.

Early-year setup tasks:

- Confirm your first premium payment cleared and coverage is active.
- Create a simple "year file" (digital folder or binder) for notices, plan documents, and tax forms.
- Write down the assumptions you're using for your income estimate and your guardrail buffer.
- Make a short list of "if this happens, we update the Marketplace" triggers tailored to your household (new job income, a move, a marriage/divorce, a coverage offer).

That last item is more powerful than it sounds. It turns "Should we report this?" into "This is on our trigger list; yes." Decision fatigue is the real enemy here.

One rule that prevents headaches: keep a running year-to-date income note, not because you love spreadsheets, but because your memory will lie to you in October. Humans remember stories, not totals.

Season 2: Monitoring and mid-course corrections (March–August)

By spring, the plan is familiar enough that it disappears into the background—which is exactly when income drift happens. A few dividends here, a consulting invoice there, a sale you didn't think about as "income," and suddenly the year has a personality you didn't plan for.

Set two check-ins on your calendar: one around late spring and one around late summer. The point is not to be precise; it's to notice direction.

What to review at each check-in:

- Year-to-date totals for the income sources most likely to drift (dividends, interest, realized gains, self-employment).
- Any intentional income moves you've already made (conversions, asset sales).
- Whether you're still inside the guardrails you set.

The surprisingly effective part is writing down a one-sentence decision after each check-in:

- "Conversions continue as planned."
- "Pause conversions until we see year-end distributions."
- "We have room to realize a planned gain."

That sentence becomes your future self's protection against impulsive December decisions.

Season 3: Open enrollment as a disciplined buying event (fall)

Open enrollment tends to collide with everything else people do in late fall: travel, holidays, end-of-year giving, and the general "how is it already November?" feeling. A checklist keeps it from becoming a rushed purchase made under seasonal stress.

Pre-open-enrollment prep (30 minutes, once):

- List your must-have providers and facilities.
- List current medications, dosages, and preferred pharmacies.
- Note your preferred plan style (e.g., lower deductible versus lower premium) and your worst-case comfort number.
- Update your income estimate for the coming year using the same guardrails approach you've used all year.

Then shop with intent. HealthCare.gov explains that automatic re-enrollment may occur if you don't act. That's a safety net to prevent a coverage gap, not a strategy for getting the best plan or the right financial help.

One extra habit pays dividends: after you choose, download or save whatever confirmation the Marketplace provides and the plan summary documents you relied on. If a network dispute or billing confusion shows up later, "I'm pretty sure I enrolled" is not the level of certainty you want.

Season 4: Tax season close-out (January–April)

Tax season is where the year's estimate meets the year's reality. If advance payments were made on your behalf, you're required to reconcile them on your tax return. This is not optional housekeeping; it's a compliance step that protects your ability to receive advance help in future years.

Two forms matter operationally:

- Form 1095-A: provides Marketplace coverage, premium, and subsidy information.

- Form 8962: used to reconcile advance payments with the amount you qualified for based on your actual household income and size.

HealthCare.gov and IRS materials are clear: Form 1095-A is used to complete Form 8962. If Form 1095-A is missing, retrieve it from your Marketplace account or contact the Marketplace.

This is also where a less-known risk lives: the failure-to-file-and-reconcile (FTR) rule. 45 CFR 155.305 limits eligibility for advance help when a tax filer (or a spouse, for married couples) fails to file and reconcile for required prior years. CMS FAQ explains the move to a 2-consecutive-tax-year standard for ineligibility in more recent rules. The practical implication is blunt: if reconciliation doesn't happen, future coverage can become dramatically more expensive overnight because you may lose access to advance help.

A good checklist treats reconciliation as a "never miss" item, like making the mortgage payment. You can debate many aspects of insurance strategy; you cannot debate filing your tax return correctly and on time.

The paperwork that actually matters (and the pile that doesn't)

One reason people hate this process is the fear of drowning in documents. The fix is to be selective: save the few items that solve real problems, and let the rest go.

Worth saving (high value):

- Eligibility and redetermination notices (they explain why your numbers changed).
- Proof of enrollment and plan selection confirmation.
- Monthly premium invoices and proof of payment (especially if autopay fails).
- Form 1095-A (and any corrected 1095-A versions).

- Your final year-end income estimate notes (what you assumed, what changed).

Usually safe to discard (low value): glossy marketing inserts and repetitive plan mailers that contain no new terms.

This isn't about minimalism for its own sake. It's about being able to answer a question in ten minutes instead of ten hours when something goes sideways.

A "one-page dashboard" that reduces 80% of the stress

If you want an unusually high return on a small organizational effort, create one page—digital or paper—with these items:

- Marketplace login location and recovery email/phone used.
- Current plan name, effective date, member IDs, insurer phone number.
- Your chosen annual MAGI target zone and guardrail buffer.
- A running estimate of year-to-date income for the volatile categories you monitor.
- Key dates: open enrollment window reminder, mid-year check-ins, tax filing deadline reminder.

The value of this page is psychological. It turns the system from "mysterious and sprawling" into "contained and checkable." It also makes it easier for a spouse or partner to step in if one person usually handles the administration.

What to do if you're self-employed, semi-retired, or otherwise income-flexible

Households with flexible income can run the year like a cockpit, not a surprise party. The checklist is the same, but the "monitoring" season becomes more active because you have real dials to turn.

Two tactical additions:

- Add a monthly (or at least quarterly) "income steering" moment: decide whether to accelerate, delay, or cap elective income moves such as conversions or optional work.
- Keep a "do not cross without a decision" number: a MAGI level beyond which you stop making elective income moves until you reassess.

This is where the operating checklist earns its keep. It transforms income management from improvisation into a series of small, reversible decisions.

A checklist you can copy: the annual operating playbook

This is intentionally short. If it's long, you won't use it.

Timing	*Do this*
January	Confirm coverage is active; first premium paid; save plan documents and proof of enrollment; create the year folder.
February	Write down your income estimate assumptions and guardrail buffer; set calendar reminders for check-ins and open enrollment.
Late spring	Update year-to-date income totals; decide whether elective income moves continue, pause, or accelerate.
Late summer	Repeat the income check; if the year is drifting, adjust elective moves; if a trigger event occurred, report it promptly.
Open enrollment week 1	Update application details; compare plans using total annual cost logic (premium + expected out-of-pocket + worst-case exposure); confirm providers and medications.
Open enrollment week 2	Enroll actively (don't rely on auto-renewal); download confirmation and plan summary documents.
January (next year)	Retrieve Form 1095-A when available; check for corrections; file taxes and reconcile using Form 8962.

Notice what's absent: perfection. There's no step that says "predict income flawlessly." There's no step that says "read every plan brochure." The list is designed around the few actions that prevent the expensive, aggravating outcomes: misaligned advance help, losing a provider unexpectedly, missing a critical tax document, or triggering FTR problems.

The real win: insurance administration stops being a recurring emergency

Marketplace coverage asks you to be a light-touch operator: forecast with humility, monitor without obsession, update promptly when reality changes, shop with discipline, and reconcile like a professional.

That sounds like a lot until you realize the alternative is worse: a year spent reacting. A repeatable operating checklist buys back your attention. And attention—especially in the years you've worked hard to reclaim—might be the most valuable asset you have.

Chapter 6

Edge Cases, Risk Management, and Confident Decision-Making

Most ACA strategies look clean on paper. Real life is not. A consulting check shows up late, a spouse changes jobs, a move resets your plan options, or income falls below the level you expected. This chapter is about staying calm when the plan gets messy: understanding the risks that matter, spotting trouble early, and making the kind of small, timely adjustments that keep healthcare costs from turning into expensive surprises.

6.1 Low-Income Risk, Medicaid Boundaries, and Coverage Disruptions

Most people approach ACA planning with one fear: "*make too much money, lose the subsidy, get a nasty surprise at tax time*". That fear is real, but it's only half the map. The other half is quieter and, for many households, more disruptive: "*earning too little*".

That sounds like a good problem to have—until you remember how Marketplace assistance is built. Premium tax credits are designed for people with *enough* income to be in the tax system in a particular way, and Medicaid is designed for people below certain income limits in a way that depends on where they live. If your year ends with income lower than you planned, the consequences aren't just financial. They can become procedural: eligibility switches, verification letters, plan termination risk, or a scramble to prove something you can't prove because the "something" never happened.

The goal isn't to hit a bullseye. The goal is to stay out of the swampy borderlands where your coverage can change for reasons that don't feel like "health insurance reasons" at all.

The uncomfortable truth: income has a floor as well as a ceiling

The Marketplace asks for an estimate of annual household income because it needs a number to calculate your advance premium tax credit (APTC)—the subsidy that can lower your monthly premium right now. But APTC is only the front end of the story. The back end is your tax return, where the premium tax credit is reconciled using Form 8962, and the question becomes brutally simple: *based on your actual annual household income, were you eligible for the credit you received in advance?*

That's where the floor matters. In broad terms, Marketplace premium tax credits have historically been tied to household income falling within a band measured as a percentage of the federal poverty level (FPL). The exact rules include exceptions and year-specific policy changes, but the planning reality is stable: there is a zone where you expected Marketplace help, but your final income can drop into a range that makes Marketplace assistance harder to justify and sometimes harder to keep.

This creates a strange early-retirement hazard. You can do everything *"right"* from a lifestyle perspective—spend modestly, keep taxes low, avoid big realized gains—and accidentally walk your income estimate down until you're no longer standing on Marketplace ground.

If that feels backwards, it is. But it's also predictable, which makes it manageable.

Why this hits early retirees in particular

Workers with paychecks are dragged across the year by W-2 gravity: every pay period adds income whether they think about it or not. A household living off savings is different. You can go months without creating much taxable income, especially if you're spending from basis, drawing from Roth contributions, or using a pile of already-taxed cash.

That flexibility is usually a superpower for subsidy planning. It also means income can quietly *fail to happen*. A consulting project gets delayed. A dividend fund pays less than expected. A planned Roth conversion gets skipped because markets are down and it "feels like a bad time." You intended to realize a small amount of capital gains, but the account is showing losses. You expected part-time work, then decide you don't need the hassle.

Each decision is sensible in isolation. Together they can pull your year-end income below the threshold you assumed would keep your Marketplace plan and subsidy stable.

The most dangerous version of this is psychological: the story that "lower income is always safer." In ACA land, lower income can be safer—until it isn't.

Medicaid is not one program, and "the line" is not in the same place everywhere

Medicaid is the elephant near the Marketplace. The ACA envisioned Medicaid covering low-income adults broadly and the Marketplace covering those above that range. In practice, states differ. Some states expanded Medicaid eligibility (creating a wider on-ramp into Medicaid for adults). Others did not, creating what's often called a *coverage gap*—a zone where income can be too low for Marketplace subsidies yet not low enough to qualify for Medicaid under that state's rules.

You don't need to memorize legal thresholds to plan well, but you do need one mindset shift: *your state's rules change what "too low" means.* Two households with the same income can have completely different outcomes depending on their address.

That's why the "income floor" is not merely a math concept. It's a geography concept. Crossing a line can mean:

- a switch from Marketplace eligibility to Medicaid eligibility (in expansion states), or
- a fall into a gap where Marketplace subsidies may not work the way you expected (in non-expansion states).

Either way, the experience can be disruptive: new paperwork, new provider networks, plan changes, and timing issues. Even when the end result is good coverage at low cost, the transition itself can be bumpy.

The real risk is churn: coverage that changes because paperwork changes

Even people who qualify cleanly for Medicaid can experience churn—coverage flipping on and off because eligibility is reassessed, documents are requested, or a file gets stuck. The last few years have provided a national reminder that administrative processes can be as consequential as eligibility rules. The lesson for an early retiree is practical: don't assume that being "eligible" automatically means being "covered without interruption."

For Marketplace households, churn shows up differently. A data mismatch notice might ask you to prove income you projected but haven't earned yet. Or you may get nudged toward Medicaid screening. Or your Marketplace savings could be reduced or suspended if verification isn't completed on time.

None of this is a judgment on your honesty. It's the system doing what systems do: comparing what you typed into an application with what shows up in databases, then asking you to reconcile the gap.

So the planning challenge becomes: *how do I keep my income plan from drifting into a range that triggers churn?*

Low-income risk often starts with a "good" decision

The easiest way to understand low-income risk is to look at the kinds of choices that create it:

You choose not to do the Roth conversion. Markets are down, and converting feels like paying tax on depressed values for no reason. The choice may be correct for long-term wealth. But if that conversion was also your "income stabilizer" for ACA purposes, skipping it can knock out a key support beam.

You harvest losses instead of gains. Tax-loss harvesting can be smart. But a year with net capital losses is a year with less income than you planned—especially if you expected to realize a measured amount of gains.

You spend from the wrong pocket (for ACA purposes). Sometimes you reach for cash reserves or Roth contributions because it feels clean and painless. It can be. It can also leave your tax return oddly quiet.

Work doesn't show up on schedule. A part-time gig starts in March instead of January, or ends early. The income shortfall is real, and it's not evenly spread across the year.

The common thread is that none of these are "mistakes." They're normal financial behavior. The fix isn't to become rigid; it's to build a margin so your best decisions don't accidentally trigger your worst administrative problems.

Your safety margin is a feature, not a fudge factor

People who like clean spreadsheets often resist buffers. A buffer feels like sloppiness. In ACA planning, a buffer is professionalism.

Think of your annual income plan like planning a road trip in winter. You don't aim to arrive with the gas tank on zero because the math says you can. You aim to arrive with a comfortable remainder because weather and detours exist. Income planning is the same. You want a cushion above whatever minimum keeps your coverage and subsidies functioning the way you intend.

Practically, this means setting a target income range rather than a single number. You already do this on the high side—staying under a cap you don't want to exceed. Do it on the low side too.

A helpful way to frame it:

- *Floor:* the level below which your plan gets administratively fragile.
- *Comfort band:* a range where normal surprises don't force action.
- *Ceiling:* the level above which you start trading away subsidies or other goals.

The comfort band is where you want to live. It lets you respond to life without turning every decision into a subsidy emergency.

Forecasting: treat income like a living estimate, not a New Year's resolution

The Marketplace application is not a one-and-done artifact. It's more like a thermostat setting. You set it, the system runs on it, and if conditions change you adjust it.

A practical rhythm is to update your year-to-date numbers and year-end projection regularly enough that you still have time to act. Quarterly works for many households. Monthly can be better if your income is lumpy or you're deliberately steering MAGI.

What matters is the *sequence*:

1. Track what has actually happened so far (income sources that count in MAGI, not just "money that arrived").
2. Update your forecast for the rest of the year using conservative assumptions.
3. Compare the projected year-end income to your comfort band.
4. If you're below the band, use an income lever that you control.

The emotional shift is the key: you're not "failing" because you need to add income. You're choosing stability—like paying for a locking gas cap after someone siphoned your tank once.

The early-warning signs of a low-income problem

Low-income risk rarely arrives as a single dramatic event. It usually leaks in through small clues:

- You notice you're spending freely but taxable income is strangely low.
- Your investments are flat or down, so capital gains are not materializing.
- You keep postponing a planned transaction that would have created income (a conversion, a gain realization, a distribution).
- You receive a Marketplace notice asking for proof of income, or indicating a data matching issue.
- You find yourself thinking, "If I just do nothing, it'll probably work out."

That last one is the trap. "Do nothing" is often the one choice that can't be corrected in December if the year is already over. If you finish the tax year below the floor, you can't go back and manufacture income for last year.

Income levers that can lift you back into the safe zone

You don't need exotic tactics. You need a short list of levers that are (1) legal, (2) controllable late in the year, and (3) likely to count in MAGI.

Common levers include:

Roth conversions (partial, measured). For many early retirees, this is the cleanest steering wheel. It creates taxable income without requiring you to sell something at a bad time or take on work you don't want. The amount is under your control, and it can be done late in the year once you have better information.

Realizing capital gains intentionally. If you hold appreciated assets in a taxable account, realizing a small amount of gains can increase income. This lever depends on market conditions and on whether you actually have gains available. It's not always there, but when it is, it can be elegant.

Traditional IRA distributions (even if you don't "need" the money). Sometimes a small distribution is the simplest fix. You can always hold the proceeds in cash for future spending or reinvest in a taxable account, depending on your broader plan.

Taking additional self-employment or part-time income. This works when it works, but it's the least controllable lever because it depends on clients, scheduling, and your willingness to trade time for income. It can be a great stabilizer if you already have the pipeline.

Each lever has tax consequences, and each interacts with your overall plan. The point here is not to prescribe a favorite; it's to avoid being stuck with *no* lever when the calendar is running out.

Conservative forecasting: the most boring tool is often the most powerful

Optimism is expensive in ACA planning. Conservative forecasting is cheap insurance.

Conservative forecasting means:

- Assume dividends and capital gains will be *lower* than last year unless you have strong reasons.
- Treat speculative income (a possible project, a maybe bonus, a potential sale) as optional until it's signed and scheduled.
- Count only what you can reasonably control when building the floor of your plan.

This is not about pessimism; it's about avoiding a particular kind of regret: the regret of discovering in March that last year's income never crossed the line, and now you're stuck solving it with paperwork instead of planning.

A subtle but crucial distinction: "income happened" vs. "income is provable"

Marketplace systems don't just care whether income is likely. They sometimes care whether it is documentable.

If you're projecting self-employment income, for example, the Marketplace may request proof. If the proof is "my best guess," that may not satisfy the request. If the proof is a signed contract, recent invoices, a letter explaining expected work and pay, or a trail of deposits, you're in a different position.

This matters for low-income risk because the time you're most likely to face verification is also the time you're least likely to have tidy proof: your income is low, irregular, or planned-but-not-yet-earned.

So part of building a margin is building a *paper* margin—choosing income levers that come with clean documentation, and keeping records as you go.

What to do if your income really is going to be low

Sometimes the right answer is: yes, income will be low, and that's okay. The planning then shifts from "prevent low income" to "prevent disruption."

A practical approach:

Update your Marketplace application promptly. If your income projection changes materially, update it rather than hoping it averages out. The goal is to reduce the odds of a large mismatch later and to keep your eligibility determination aligned with reality.

Prepare for the possibility of program handoffs. In expansion states, a lower income projection may push you toward Medicaid eligibility. That can be a good outcome financially. The question becomes whether you are comfortable with Medicaid's provider networks and administrative cadence. If you're not, this is the moment to slow down and plan your next moves deliberately.

Avoid accidental "zero income" optics. Many retirees can live for a long time on accounts that don't create taxable income. If your plan results in extremely low reported income, be ready for the system to ask, in effect, "how are you paying your bills?" This doesn't mean you did something wrong. It means your file looks unusual. A clear explanation and consistent records help.

Keep an eye on deadlines. Verification requests and data matching issues often come with a clock. Missing the clock can cause loss of savings or coverage even if your situation is otherwise legitimate.

Low income isn't the enemy. Surprise low income is.

The "Medicaid boundary" problem: your doctor may care more than your wallet

The hardest part of Medicaid transitions is rarely the premium. It's continuity: doctors, prescriptions, and ongoing treatment.

A household can be financially thrilled and medically frustrated at the same time. If you're managing a chronic condition, seeing specialists, or taking medications that are finicky about coverage, a midstream network change can feel like a rug pull.

That's why the income floor is not purely a subsidy optimization game. It's a continuity game. Keeping your Marketplace plan stable—when it's working well for your providers—can be worth paying a bit more in taxes than you otherwise would, simply to avoid swapping systems unexpectedly.

This is a personal trade-off, not a universal rule. But it's one that deserves to be made consciously rather than as the accidental consequence of "we ended up with a quiet tax return."

Building a "minimum viable income" plan

A useful mental model is to build a minimum viable income plan at the start of the year: a short script of actions you can take if income is trending low.

It might look like:

- If projected income is within a small margin of the floor by the end of Q2, execute a partial Roth conversion of $X.
- If markets are down and gains aren't available, use conversion/distribution levers instead of relying on capital gains.
- If a consulting project is delayed, don't wait for it to rescue the year; treat it as upside, not base.

The value of a minimum viable plan is that it removes drama. You're not improvising under pressure; you're executing a policy you chose while calm.

Why "I'll fix it in December" is a risky philosophy

December fixing works best for issues where you control the lever and the numbers. Low-income risk has two features that make last-minute fixes fragile:

First, some income can't be summoned on command. Work income needs clients. Capital gains need gains. Rental income needs tenants.

Second, December is when life gets busy. Travel, family obligations, holidays, end-of-year business closures, and simple fatigue all pile up. The plan that requires perfect execution on December 28 is the plan most likely to fail.

A better approach is to create an "action window" earlier—late summer or early fall—when you still have time to correct course if the first correction doesn't land exactly where you expected.

A practical way to choose your buffer size

People want a precise buffer number. The honest answer is that the "right" buffer depends on how volatile your income is and how costly disruption would be for your household.

A simple way to calibrate:

If your income is predictable and your coverage can tolerate change, the buffer can be smaller. Example: you have stable pension income, minimal investment volatility in taxable accounts, and no strong provider network attachment.

If your income is unpredictable or a plan change would be medically painful, the buffer should be larger. Example: you're relying on irregular consulting income, or you have ongoing care with providers you don't want to lose.

The buffer is not just about money. It's about friction. The more you dislike paperwork, rushed phone calls, and mid-year plan churn, the more you should pay for stability with a wider margin.

What "coverage disruption" looks like in real life

It's easy to imagine disruption as a dramatic cancellation letter. More often it's death by a thousand cuts:

- Premiums suddenly increase because savings were adjusted.
- You get a notice that says benefits may change if documents aren't submitted.
- A prescription refill gets delayed because the plan changed or the pharmacy needs new billing information.
- You spend hours on hold to confirm that your plan is still active, then hours more uploading documents that you already have in a folder somewhere.

The cost is partly financial, but the bigger cost is cognitive. Retirement is supposed to reduce noise. Administrative chaos is noise.

A well-designed income floor is one of the quieter forms of wealth: it buys you fewer interruptions.

The mindset that makes this easy: buy yourself options

High-income risk is about avoiding accidental consequences. Low-income risk is about avoiding accidental *constraints*.

When income ends up lower than planned, you don't just lose dollars—you can lose options. The system may push you toward Medicaid. Your Marketplace savings may become uncertain. Your providers may become uncertain. Your timeline becomes uncertain.

The antidote is to keep at least one lever in reserve that you can pull without needing anyone's permission: a conversion, a distribution, a planned transaction you can execute cleanly and document.

That's the core of confident decision-making here. Not perfect prediction. Not heroic spreadsheeting. Just a calm recognition that in ACA planning, "too low" is a real place—and you're going to stay comfortably away from it on purpose.

6.2 Consulting, Gig Work, and Uneven Income in Early Retirement

A steady paycheck is boring in the best way. It arrives on schedule, it withholds taxes quietly, and it makes your annual income estimate a low-drama exercise.

Consulting and gig work are the opposite: exciting, flexible, and allergic to calendars. Income comes in bursts, expenses arrive in clumps, and the line between "business" and "life" can blur at exactly the wrong moment—like the week you also need to update your ACA application.

The trick is not to turn yourself into an accountant. The trick is to run a simple control panel that keeps two truths visible at all times: what your work is doing to your tax return *and* what it's doing to your health insurance savings.

Uneven income doesn't just change totals; it changes timing, and timing is where ACA stress lives

The ACA asks you to predict a full-year number, then hands you monthly savings based on that prediction. Self-employment income rarely behaves like a tidy annual salary, so your estimate will be wrong at least part of the year. That's not a failure; it's the normal shape of the problem.

The risk comes from letting "wrong for now" become "wrong all year." If you guess low early, take a large APTC all year, then land a big project in November, the system doesn't retroactively re-price your earlier months. It keeps moving forward, then settles up on your tax return. That settle-up happens through Form 8962, and IRS Pub. 974 and the Form 8962 instructions are the reference manuals for how that reconciliation works. The practical translation: if APTC exceeds the credit you're allowed based on actual annual results, the excess can increase tax owed or reduce your refund. If APTC was too small, you may be able to claim additional credit.

That is a good system for people with stable income. For people with lumpy income, it's a system that rewards mid-year course corrections.

A useful mental model: you are running two ledgers

If you do contract work, you are already running a business, even if it's just you and a laptop. That business runs two ledgers:

Ledger 1: the business ledger. What came in, what went out, and what counts as a legitimate business expense.

Ledger 2: the ACA ledger. What your year-to-date numbers imply about year-end MAGI, and what that implies for your APTC and cost-sharing plan.

Most headaches happen when these ledgers are kept in different mental rooms. You buy a plane ticket for a client trip and log it as an expense (business ledger), but you don't notice that the project payment shifted into next year (ACA ledger). You celebrate the deduction and forget the missing revenue—until you get an eligibility notice or a tax-time surprise.

Putting both ledgers on the same dashboard is the adult version of "don't lose the receipt." It's not about compliance for compliance's sake. It's about staying in control of a system that will otherwise reconcile you at the worst possible time.

Gross revenue is not income (and your ACA estimate should respect that)

One common early mistake is to treat revenue as if it were your income. That's understandable: money lands in the bank account; it feels like income.

But self-employment has friction. Some of that friction is legitimate business expense. Some of it is tax. Some of it is simply the reality that a $10,000 invoice is not a $10,000 lifestyle upgrade.

For ACA planning, what you care about is where your MAGI is headed. The exact components are tax-return mechanics, but the practical workflow is consistent:

- track revenue as it arrives,
- track deductible expenses as they happen,
- maintain a rolling projection of net profit (or loss),
- and translate that projection into your annual income estimate for ACA purposes.

This is where self-employed households can be accidentally reckless in both directions. Some people ignore expenses and overestimate income, leaving subsidies on the table. Others assume the business will "work out" and underestimate income, then take more APTC than they ultimately qualify for.

The cure is not perfection. The cure is updating your projection often enough that no single month gets to define the year.

The "big expense month" problem: deductions that arrive before the work does

Gig work has a classic trap: you spend money to earn money, but the money you earn arrives later.

A new laptop in January. Software subscriptions all billed annually. Travel booked upfront. A marketing push that produces clients slowly. That can make your year-to-date net income look low (or negative) even if you're on track for a healthy year.

Low year-to-date income can tempt you into two moves that don't play nicely together:

- lowering your income estimate aggressively, and

- taking the full calculated APTC.

Then April to August arrives, the invoices start landing, and suddenly your year-end income is trending far above your early estimate. At that point, the system isn't "wrong." It's doing what you asked with the information you gave it. The problem is that you treated temporary timing as permanent reality.

A practical fix is to keep a separate line on your dashboard for *one-time or front-loaded expenses* and annotate them. Not because you can't deduct them, but because you don't want a January purchase to bully your annual income forecast.

Documentation is part of the job now (and it doesn't need to be painful)

Marketplace verification requests often focus on income because income is the hinge for eligibility. For W-2 workers, pay stubs do the talking. For consultants, the story is more nuanced.

You can make that story easy to tell by keeping a thin but credible paper trail:

- signed contracts or emails confirming rate and expected hours,
- invoices sent and paid,
- a simple income-and-expense spreadsheet updated monthly,
- receipts for major expenses with a short note ("client travel," "software for project X").

This isn't "gaming" an estimate. It's supporting a reasonable projection. If the Marketplace asks why your application says $45,000 but your year-to-date bank deposits are lower, your answer is more convincing when it comes with dates, documents, and a calm explanation of timing.

The irony is that a little documentation makes you more flexible. You can take gigs opportunistically without worrying that a later verification request will turn into a scavenger hunt.

Estimated taxes: the silent partner that can wreck your numbers if you ignore it

Self-employment creates a second kind of mismatch: you can have a great year on paper and still be short of liquidity because you forgot taxes.

Quarterly estimated taxes are not an ACA concept, but they interact with ACA planning because they affect your willingness to take income. If you avoid a late-year Roth conversion or a profitable gig because you're afraid of the tax bill, you've handed the steering wheel to anxiety.

A cleaner approach is to treat estimated taxes as part of your operating system:

- set aside a portion of each client payment for taxes the day it arrives,
- keep that money in a separate bucket (even a separate savings account),
- and revisit the percentage as your year-end projection becomes clearer.

This is not about being conservative for its own sake. It's about keeping your income levers usable. The ability to accept work or realize income without panic is a form of financial strength—and it makes your ACA decisions calmer.

The APTC dial: a buffer that buys you sleep

There's an underused tool for uneven income: you can choose to take *less* APTC than the Marketplace calculates.

That choice is not a moral stance. It's a risk-management stance.

If your income is volatile, taking the maximum APTC is like driving a mountain road with your headlights off because you "probably know the turns." You might be fine. Or you might round a corner into a November project that makes your annual income much higher than predicted, and now the tax return is where you discover the consequences.

Some households deliberately set their APTC to a fraction of what they're offered—think "APTC at 70%"—and treat the remaining subsidy as a tax-time bonus if it turns out they were eligible for more. This approach lines up with what IRS guidance emphasizes in plain language: changes in income can make APTC too high, and reporting changes to the Marketplace during the year can reduce the risk of a large tax-time adjustment. Taking less APTC is another way to reduce that risk.

The trade-off is obvious: higher monthly premiums in exchange for fewer surprises. For consultants, fewer surprises can be worth real money, because surprises often arrive in the same season as final estimated taxes and year-end business chaos.

A concrete scenario: the "November project" that changes everything

Picture a semi-retired consultant who expects $45,000 of annual MAGI. They choose a plan and take APTC sized for that estimate. Through October, business is quiet. Then in November, a former client calls with an urgent $20,000 project.

That project is good news—unless it's handled as an afterthought.

There are three reasonable responses, and the best one depends on temperament:

Option A: update the Marketplace estimate promptly. This can reduce APTC going forward and shrink the tax-time gap. It won't rewrite earlier months, but it can keep the final numbers closer to reality. IRS guidance explicitly encourages reporting changes during the year to reduce the risk of a large tax-time adjustment.

Option B: keep the estimate but reduce APTC going forward. Some people prefer not to churn the application repeatedly. Dialing down APTC without fully reworking the estimate can still reduce repayment risk. It's a practical compromise: fewer administrative steps, but a nod to reality.

Option C: keep everything as-is and prepare for Form 8962 reconciliation. This can be fine if you have the money set aside and you prefer simplicity now over optimization. It becomes dangerous if you treat it as "free money" and spend it.

The wrong move is the common one: do nothing, hope the math is kind, and then act shocked in April.

Prospective changes: why speed matters even though the year is annual

One frustrating part of ACA mechanics is that redeterminations are generally implemented prospectively after notice and verification timing. That means an update today mostly affects future months, not past months.

That might sound like "updates don't matter much," but the opposite is true. If you wait until December to reflect a major income increase that actually happened in July, you may have taken too much APTC for months. Updating sooner reduces the span of the mismatch. It's the difference between "a small correction" and "a season-long drift."

Speed is a form of kindness to your future self.

Business deductions: use them, but don't let them become a storytelling problem

Deductions are legitimate. They're also misunderstood.

A well-run solo business might have expenses that swing wildly month to month. That's normal. What's not normal is letting those swings become a narrative that's hard to defend. If your income estimate implies a modest year but you're billing heavily and buying equipment aggressively, an automated system may flag the mismatch.

The simplest way to keep deductions from turning into drama is to separate:

- *recurring operating expenses* (software, supplies, mileage, small tools), and
- *punctuation-mark expenses* (a new computer, a major trip, a multi-year membership).

Punctuation-mark expenses are not suspicious. They're just memorable. They deserve a note, a receipt, and a quick sentence in your own records: what it was for, and why it happened *this year*. If you later need to explain income volatility, you'll be glad you wrote the sentence while you still remember.

Treat your projection like a weather report: update it, don't marry it

A good income projection is humble. It changes with new information.

One practical habit: every month (or quarter, if your work is steadier), write down three numbers:

1. year-to-date revenue,
2. year-to-date deductible business expenses,
3. projected net for the year.

Then add a short note: "What would have to happen for this projection to be wrong?"

That note is surprisingly powerful. It forces you to acknowledge what you're assuming:

- "Assumes client X renews in September."
- "Assumes no additional travel."
- "Assumes project Y ends in July."

Assumptions are not bad. Hidden assumptions are.

A simple dashboard table you can actually maintain

Many people abandon tracking systems because they're too ambitious. The cure is to track fewer things, more consistently.

Dashboard item	*What you're trying to learn*
YTD business revenue	Is work arriving as expected, or is the year taking a new shape?
YTD business expenses (deductible)	Are expenses normal, front-loaded, or unusually high-/low?
Projected year-end net profit	What does your business likely contribute to annual MAGI?
Non-business income forecast	Are dividends/interest/other income sources behaving as planned?
APTC setting (full vs reduced)	Are you choosing stability now, or optimizing month by month?
Tax set-aside balance	Can you say "yes" to income without fearing the tax bill?

This table is intentionally plain. It's not a bookkeeping system. It's a decision system.

The emotional pitfall: treating gig income as "bonus money"

Flexible work often arrives with a mental label: "extra." That label is comforting, but it can be misleading.

For ACA planning, "extra" income is still income. It changes MAGI, which changes the amount of credit you're ultimately eligible for. If you treat gig income as play money and ignore its effect on your annual numbers, you can end up paying back subsidies with the very income that was supposed to be fun.

A better label is "variable income." Variable income isn't automatically dangerous; it's simply income that requires a response. The response might be updating your Marketplace estimate, adjusting your APTC dial, increasing your tax set-aside, or choosing to stop accepting new projects once you hit your comfort range.

Notice what's missing: guilt. This is not about whether you "should" work. It's about making work a tool instead of a surprise.

How to stop working mid-year without creating an eligibility mess

Another common consulting pattern is the intentional pause: you take projects in spring, then you're done.

That's a great lifestyle design. It can be an ACA headache if your application assumes that spring income continues all year. The fix is straightforward, but it requires follow-through: update your income projection once you know the work is ending. If the Marketplace asks for income verification, you're in a much stronger position if you can document that the contract ended, the client stopped sending work, or you're shifting to zero billable hours.

This is also where conservative forecasting helps. If you assume "some work might happen in the fall" and it doesn't, you can drift toward the low-income boundary. If you assume "no work after June" and then you land an October project, that's a happier surprise to manage.

Make irregular work serve your plan, not sabotage it

The best part of consulting and gig work is that it's adjustable. You can take more, take less, take only high-value work, or take work that fits your life. That flexibility is rare.

Used well, it becomes an elegant planning lever:

- If your income projection is low, you can accept a small project and solve the problem with labor rather than financial gymnastics.
- If your projection is high, you can decline work and protect subsidies without feeling deprived—because you're trading work for savings, and that's a rational trade.
- If your year is trending unpredictable, you can take less APTC and treat tax-time reconciliation as the moment you settle up cleanly, on your terms.

The bigger point is that uneven income isn't a defect to be tolerated. It's a resource to be managed. With a modest dashboard, a tax set-aside habit, and the willingness to adjust your estimate during the year, flexible work stops being "messy money" and starts being one of the most useful knobs you have.

6.3 Marriage, Divorce, Moves, and Other Mid-Year Household Changes

The ACA Marketplace is a little like a flight reservation system: it can handle a lot of change, but it hates surprises. Household facts—who's in the household, where you live, who has other coverage available, and what income you expect for the year—are the inputs. If the inputs change and the file doesn't, the system doesn't politely ask for clarification at tax time. It just keeps charging the premium you were quoted and sending the subsidy you asked for. Then the reconciliation machinery shows up later with a calculator and no interest in your backstory.

The clean way to live with this is to treat household changes as *trigger events* with a response script. Not a 20-step emergency plan—a short, practiced sequence that you can run even while dealing with, you know, an actual divorce or a cross-country move.

The two clocks that matter: enrollment clock and reconciliation clock

Household changes run on two clocks at once, and confusing them is how smart people end up with dumb outcomes.

Clock 1 is the enrollment clock. Certain events can unlock a Special Enrollment Period (SEP), which is your window to enroll or change plans outside open enrollment. That window is often limited (commonly 60 days after the event), and some events come with extra conditions or documentation expectations.

Clock 2 is the reconciliation clock. The subsidy is ultimately reconciled for the taxable year. If your household size ends up smaller than what you reported, IRS guidance highlights that APTC may be higher than allowed, increasing the risk of paying some back. If your income ends up higher, same story. If your plan year and your life year don't match, the tax return is where the mismatch gets priced.

The enrollment clock is about getting covered correctly *now*. The reconciliation clock is about not getting billed *later*. You want to satisfy both.

The fastest way to get into trouble: assuming "life event = automatic fix"

People assume the system "knows" what happened. Your insurer knows you moved because your mail gets forwarded. Your employer knows you got married because you changed your benefits. Your ex knows you got divorced because, well, that was the point.

The Marketplace doesn't know anything unless you tell it. HealthCare.gov explicitly instructs consumers to report life changes including income, household members, and address because those changes can affect plan options and APTC/CSR eligibility. That's not a suggestion; it's operational reality. If you don't update, the Marketplace will continue to act as if your household facts are frozen in time.

A frozen file is comfortable for about three weeks. Then it starts costing you money or creating paperwork.

A response script that works for almost any household change

Household changes can be emotionally loud. The response script should be emotionally quiet. Here's a practical order that keeps the chaos contained:

1. *Identify the event date.* Not "sometime in April." A date. The SEP and documentation often care about a date.
2. *Ask: did anyone gain or lose other coverage?* This can determine whether you even have an SEP and what your options are.
3. *Update the Marketplace file promptly.* Household members, address, income projection, and coverage offers should match reality.
4. *Re-shop plans with a narrow goal.* Not "find the best plan on Earth." Find a plan that covers the right people, in the right place, with the right networks, at a subsidy level that matches the new year-end picture.
5. *Save proof and confirmations.* If something goes sideways later, your best friend is a timestamped record.

If that looks too simple, good. Complexity is not your friend during a move, a marriage, or a breakup.

Marriage: the happiest paperwork you'll ever do (and it can still bite)

Marriage can change everything at once: household size, income, and the way you file taxes. It can also unlock an SEP, but it comes with nuance that surprises people who treat it as automatic.

CMS SEP guidance adds detail beyond the consumer-facing pages, including marriage SEP rules that may require prior qualifying coverage for at least one spouse for one or more days in the 60 days before the marriage (with exceptions). Translation: getting married is often a qualifying event, but it may not work the way you assume if one spouse was uninsured right before the wedding.

Even after enrollment is handled, the subsidy math can change sharply because the household income calculation shifts to the combined household. Some couples are shocked by this not because they are doing anything wrong, but because they were mentally running two separate systems. The Marketplace runs one.

A practical marriage checklist:

- Decide who will be on which coverage for the rest of the year (employer plan, Marketplace, or a mix).
- Update household and income promptly so the APTC calculation reflects the combined situation.
- Re-check provider networks. Marriage often changes where people receive care, especially if one spouse wants to keep a long-standing doctor.

Marriage is also a moment to revisit your risk posture. If the combined income is harder to predict (commissions, consulting, variable bonuses), dialing down APTC can be a sanity move. The goal is not to optimize to the penny; it's to avoid turning your first year married into a reconciliation surprise.

Divorce and legal separation: the SEP myth that causes real damage

Divorce feels like it should automatically unlock the ability to change plans. Sometimes it does. Sometimes it absolutely does not.

HealthCare.gov states a specific carve-out that catches people off guard: divorce or legal separation without losing coverage doesn't qualify for SEP. That is a deeply unintuitive rule, and it's responsible for a lot of frantic phone calls.

Why does it matter? Because divorce is often the moment households want to change everything: split coverage, change addresses, change finances. But the Marketplace cares about the precise trigger that opens the enrollment door. If you assume "divorce = SEP" and you're wrong, you might miss the real SEP window tied to the actual loss of coverage date.

A more reliable way to think about divorce is to separate it into two questions:

Question 1: who is actually losing coverage, and when? That date is often what drives the SEP. If one spouse stays on an employer plan until the decree is final, the loss-of-coverage date might be later than the emotional separation. If someone is removed from a spouse's plan mid-month, the loss can be immediate.

Question 2: what is the new household for ACA purposes for the year? Household size and filing status interact with the annual credit. IRS guidance highlights that if household size is smaller than reported, APTC may be higher than allowed. Divorce is the archetype: if the Marketplace file still shows two people but the tax return ultimately reflects one, the subsidy math can get ugly.

Divorce planning is often framed as "get coverage." The subtler win is "get coverage *and* stop the wrong APTC from running in the background."

A divorce timeline that avoids the most common mistakes

The most expensive divorce mistake in ACA land is not emotional; it's procedural: leaving the Marketplace file unchanged for months because there are more pressing fires.

A practical timeline looks like this:

- *As soon as separate households are real:* update address and household members for the Marketplace account(s) involved, even if final legal paperwork is pending.
- *As soon as coverage loss is scheduled:* line up the SEP action so coverage starts on time. Do not assume the divorce decree date is the coverage loss date.
- *As soon as income expectations change:* update the income projection. Divorce can change who claims what income, who receives spousal support, and who can rely on which assets.

This is not about being obsessive. It's about avoiding a situation where the system keeps paying APTC for a household configuration that no longer exists.

New dependent, dependent aging off, or "surprise household size"

Household size is a big lever in subsidy math. Add a person, and you may become eligible for more assistance. Lose a person, and you may discover you were receiving too much.

Most people focus on births and adoptions (obvious changes). The sneakier ones are:

- a dependent who is no longer in your tax household for the year,
- a young adult who moves out and gets their own coverage,
- shared custody arrangements where the tax dependency flips.

These changes are emotionally mundane and administratively sharp. The Marketplace file needs to match the household you expect to claim on the tax return. If it doesn't, the system keeps sending APTC based on a headcount that may not exist in April.

If the dependency situation is unclear mid-year (common with shared custody), the best strategy is to be conservative with APTC and keep excellent notes about what you reported and why. You're not aiming for perfect prophecy; you're aiming to avoid a mismatch so large that it turns into a financial shock.

A spouse takes a job mid-year: the "other coverage" trap

One of the most common mid-year shocks is simple: a spouse gets hired.

That single event can change:

- household income,
- the availability of employer-sponsored insurance,
- and whether the Marketplace plan and its APTC still make sense.

People often update the income (because that feels obvious) but forget the other coverage offer (because it feels separate). It isn't separate. The Marketplace wants to know about offers of coverage because it affects eligibility and plan strategy.

Operationally, the risk is this: if a spouse becomes eligible for employer coverage and the household continues receiving APTC as if nothing happened, the reconciliation can be painful. IRS guidance warns that changes can make APTC too high; reporting changes during the year can reduce the risk of a large tax-time adjustment. A new job is exactly such a change.

A smart response is not necessarily "everyone jumps to the employer plan tomorrow." Employer coverage may be expensive, may have a narrow network, or may not start until next month. The smart response is to update the Marketplace file promptly, then decide deliberately:

- Who stays on the Marketplace plan, if anyone?
- Does it make sense to reduce APTC as a buffer while the situation settles?
- Do you need to change plans because the household composition changed?

The enemy is the quiet drift: letting new income and new coverage offers exist in real life while the Marketplace file remains stuck in the old world.

Moves: the moment your plan discovers it is a local product

Health insurance is intensely geographic. A plan that is perfect in one county can be useless two counties over because the network is different. Moves are where people learn, abruptly, that a "national" insurer can still have a very local plan.

Moves can qualify you for an SEP, but they can come with additional requirements and documentation expectations. The Marketplace may want proof of the move date and proof of prior coverage. People who are otherwise excellent planners get tripped up here because moving already generates an avalanche of paperwork—and the health insurance paperwork is not the one that arrives in a neat envelope.

The practical move strategy is to treat health insurance as one of the moving tasks with a hard deadline:

- As soon as the move is scheduled: gather documents you'll likely have anyway (lease, closing statement, utility setup confirmation).
- Keep proof of prior coverage accessible. Don't bury it in a box labeled "Taxes."

- Update your address promptly so the Marketplace shows plans available in the new service area.

A key subtlety: even if you love your current plan, your move may force a plan change because the service area changed. That's not personal. It's how these products are built.

The "move + income change" combo event

Moves are rarely pure. People move for jobs, to downsize, to be near family, or to change cost of living. Those reasons often change income.

That combination matters because it can shift both the plans available and the subsidy level at the same time. If you update only the address, you may accidentally keep an income estimate that is no longer realistic. If you update only the income, you may be shopping plans that won't even exist in the new zip code.

The clean approach is coordinated updates: address and income together, then shop plans once the Marketplace is describing your real situation.

Speed beats perfection (and perfection is usually a delay tactic)

People procrastinate on Marketplace updates for the same reason they procrastinate on dentist appointments: they assume it will be unpleasant and time-consuming. Sometimes it is. But postponing it doesn't reduce the unpleasantness; it just adds consequences.

The most reliable habit is to separate *updating facts* from *making the final plan choice*. Updating facts is quick: the household changed, the address changed, income expectations changed, a coverage offer exists. Plan choice can take more time, especially if you need to recheck doctors or medications.

Update facts first. Then shop.

That sequence also reduces the chance of chasing phantom plans. There's nothing quite like spending an hour comparing deductibles and networks only to discover the plan isn't available in your new county.

A mini checklist of what to save for common household changes

Household-change problems often turn into documentation problems. Not because you did anything wrong, but because systems want proof.

Here's the kind of documentation that reduces friction:

- *Marriage:* marriage certificate date; proof of prior coverage (if relevant to SEP conditions); confirmation of Marketplace update.
- *Divorce/separation:* coverage termination date(s); any employer/plan notices; confirmation of Marketplace update; address change proof.
- *Move:* lease or closing paperwork; utility bill or address confirmation; proof of prior coverage; confirmation of Marketplace update.
- *New job/employer offer:* offer letter or benefits summary showing eligibility date; confirmation of Marketplace update.

You don't need a filing cabinet worthy of a law firm. You need a single folder (digital is fine) that can answer the question the Marketplace is most likely to ask: *what changed, and when?*

The calm mindset that prevents the quiet mistakes

Household changes are exactly when people want to stop thinking about admin. That's also when the admin matters most.

A useful mindset is to treat the Marketplace file as a living profile rather than a once—a-year application. Every major household change is a cue to bring the profile back into sync with reality. HealthCare.gov's guidance to report income, household member changes, and address is essentially the system begging you to do this before small mismatches become large ones.

The win isn't that your life becomes perfectly documentable. The win is that your coverage and subsidies move with your life instead of lagging behind it like an unpaid bill.

6.4 Documentation, Verification, and Resolving Marketplace Problems

The Marketplace is not a person. It doesn't "get the gist." It can't tell that you're honest, organized, and only slightly irritated. It runs on files, dates, and matching rules, and it will happily treat a missing PDF the same way it treats a lie: as unresolved.

That sounds harsh, but it's also liberating. If the system is impersonal, you don't need charm. You need a paper trail. Documentation is financial self-defense in the gap years: it protects your subsidies, reduces the odds of coverage disruption, and gives you leverage when something goes wrong.

The good news is that you don't need an accountant's archive. You need a repeatable system that produces three outcomes: (1) you can prove what you claimed, (2) you can meet deadlines without scrambling, and (3) you can escalate confidently if the Marketplace makes a bad call.

The most common Marketplace problem is not fraud. It's a mismatch

Many Marketplace headaches start with something called a *data matching issue/inconsistency* (often shortened to DMI). HealthCare.gov defines DMIs as mismatches between application information and trusted data sources. In plain language, you told the

Marketplace one thing, a database suggests another, and the system wants proof.

This can happen for mundane reasons:

- Your income dropped after leaving work, but the system is looking at last year's tax information.
- Your household changed, but another database still shows the old address.
- Your consulting income is seasonal, and the "trusted data" doesn't know your contract ended.

The danger isn't the mismatch itself. The danger is ignoring the notice. HealthCare.gov warns that unresolved inconsistencies can lead to loss of coverage or loss/adjustment of financial assistance. That's a mechanical consequence, not a moral verdict.

So the first rule is simple: treat every Marketplace notice as if it can affect your premium next month. Because it can.

Notices come with clocks, and the clock wins

HealthCare.gov's required-documents guidance emphasizes that notices specify what to submit and by when. You may hear a common timeframe mentioned (often 90 days) to resolve certain inconsistencies, but the notice controls. Your job is not to debate fairness; your job is to beat the deadline.

A quiet best practice: the day a notice arrives, extract three things and write them somewhere obvious:

1. what the Marketplace says is inconsistent,
2. what documents it says are acceptable,
3. the deadline date.

Then set a reminder for a week before the deadline and another for a few days before. The second reminder is not pessimism. It's acknowledgment of a universal truth: uploads fail, call centers disconnect, and "I'll do it tomorrow" is a powerful drug.

Build a paper trail that is small, fast, and hard to break

A good paper trail system has two features: it's easy enough that you'll actually use it, and it produces records that are persuasive to a bureaucracy.

Here's a simple structure that works well:

- *Folder 1: Marketplace.* Application PDFs, update confirmations, eligibility notices, DMI letters, screenshots of "submitted" pages.
- *Folder 2: Premiums & Coverage.* Monthly premium invoices, proof of payment, insurer ID cards, termination letters (if any).
- *Folder 3: Income Proof.* Pay stubs, offer letters, benefit letters, consulting contracts, invoices, year-to-date profit/loss summaries, documentation showing contract work ended or wages changed.
- *Folder 4: Taxes.* Form 1095-A, Form 8962, and anything you used to reconcile or explain changes.

Make each folder boring. The point is retrieval. If you can't find it in 60 seconds, the system is too complicated.

For naming files, consistency beats creativity. A format like `YYYY-MM-DD_Marketplace_Notice_IncomeDMI.pdf` feels obsessive until the day you need to prove you submitted something on time.

What to save that people rarely save (and regret later)

Everyone saves tax forms. The documents that rescue you tend to be the unglamorous ones:

Update confirmations. Every time you update the Marketplace, save the confirmation page or email. If a later notice claims you never updated, this is your receipt.

A dated call log. Create a simple text file or note with: date/time, phone number called, representative name or ID (if offered), and what they told you. It's amazing how quickly "I called three times" becomes "I have no idea who I spoke with."

Screenshots of upload success. Upload portals can be finicky. Save proof that the system accepted the document.

The "why" note. When you make a major change (income estimate drops, household member removed, move), write a one-paragraph note to yourself: what changed, and why the new estimate is reasonable. This isn't for the Marketplace; it's for Future You, who will not remember the details in six months.

This kind of record-keeping is the adult version of labeling freezer bags. It's not elegant, but it prevents waste.

Income verification: win by telling a coherent story, not by uploading random PDFs

Income verification can sound intimidating, especially for households with consulting, variable hours, or a recent retirement date. But most verification problems aren't about the number. They're about the *story*.

The Marketplace is asking, essentially: "You say your annual income will be X. Show us why that's plausible."

HealthCare.gov notes that income verification can be supported by pay stubs and other documents that reflect expected annual income, including statements about contract work ending or wage changes. That last part matters. Many early retirees have a perfectly legitimate income drop that isn't visible in last year's tax data. Your documents need to make the drop legible.

A coherent income-proof packet often includes:

- a recent pay stub or two if any wages exist,
- a letter or document showing the job ended or hours changed (employer letter, separation notice, or similar),
- for contract work: invoices and evidence of payment, plus something showing whether work is ongoing or ended (contract terms, client email, or your own dated statement describing expected hours and timeframe),
- a simple year-to-date summary that annualizes expected income in a way a stranger can follow.

You're not trying to impress anyone with sophistication. You're trying to prevent a bureaucratic person (or automated system) from concluding, "We can't verify this."

Document quality matters more than people expect

A surprising number of verification failures are not substantive. They're technical.

Before uploading, run a quick quality check:

- *Legible:* not blurry, not cut off, not photographed at an angle.
- *Name matches:* the document should clearly tie to the applicant (or spouse) by name.
- *Date visible:* the document should show a date, especially for changes like job loss or reduced hours.
- *Amount interpretable:* if you submit a pay stub, the relevant pay period and year-to-date fields should be readable.
- *Annual logic:* if the Marketplace is asking about annual income, make sure what you submit can reasonably be interpreted in annual terms (even if the document is monthly or weekly).

If you've ever watched a doctor's office reject an insurance card photo because the numbers are fuzzy, you already understand this. Bureaucracies love clarity.

A common scenario: "Our income dropped, and the system doesn't believe us"

One spouse stops working. The household income estimate drops. You update the Marketplace. Then a DMI notice arrives because the system's trusted data still reflects last year's higher income.

This is not the system accusing you of lying; it's the system saying, "The old data contradicts the new claim. Prove the change."

The clean response is to assemble a packet that makes the change undeniable:

- proof that the job ended or hours were reduced (a document with a date),
- a recent pay stub showing the new reality (or last pay stub showing final employment),
- if there is severance or unemployment income expected, include the best documentation available,
- a short written statement (one page, dated) explaining the new expected annual income and what sources remain.

That last item—a short statement—is underrated. Systems process documents; humans interpret them. Give the human a map.

Submission strategy: submit, confirm, and then confirm again

Uploading documents is not the finish line; it's the starting gun for the Marketplace to review them.

A professional cadence looks like this:

1. Submit documents through the channel specified (online upload, phone-assisted process, or in-person help).
2. Save proof of submission immediately.
3. Wait a reasonable period, then check status.
4. If the inconsistency still shows, follow up: call, reference the notice, reference the upload date, and ask what exactly is still missing.

CMS provides job aids/guides for resolving DMIs that reinforce an operational sequence: identify the issue type, gather acceptable documents, submit via the correct Marketplace channel, and confirm completion. The spirit here is methodical persistence. You're not pleading; you're closing a ticket.

If the Marketplace still shows an inconsistency after you uploaded: assume a processing problem, not a personal failure

This happens. You upload a clean document. Days pass. The DMI remains. The system may not have processed it yet, or it may have rejected it for a reason that isn't obvious.

At that point, avoid the instinct to throw more random documents at the portal. Randomness creates confusion.

Instead:

- Re-read the notice and confirm you addressed the exact issue type.
- Re-check the document quality factors (name, date, legibility, annual logic).
- Call and ask specifically whether the document was received and whether it is acceptable. If not, ask what would be acceptable *for this issue*.

- If needed, re-upload a clearer version with a short cover note embedded as the first page (a dated statement describing what you're submitting and why).

This is where your call log becomes valuable. If you speak to three representatives and receive three different answers, your log keeps you sane and gives you a factual narrative if you need to escalate.

Premium payments: the dull record that can save your coverage

Even while dealing with verification, you still have to pay premiums. It's painfully common for households to focus on the paperwork battle and accidentally miss a payment, creating a second problem on top of the first.

Save:

- the invoice,
- the payment confirmation (bank record or insurer receipt),
- any correspondence about payment processing.

If an insurer later claims a payment was missed, you want a clean timeline. This is not paranoia. It's basic defense against billing glitches and mail delays.

Escalation: the moment to stop looping and start climbing

Sometimes ordinary resolution fails. You call. You upload. You call again. The problem persists. At that point, the danger is not just the unresolved issue; it's the time you're losing.

HealthCare.gov provides an eligibility appeal process as a formal escalation path, with the ability to request records used in the determination. That's a big deal. It means there is a way to move beyond call-center roulette and ask, formally, for the basis of the decision.

Escalation is not an emotional outburst. It's a procedural move. Consider it when:

- you have submitted the requested documents and can prove it,
- deadlines are approaching and the system is not updating,
- the determination is clearly inconsistent with the facts you can document.

If you decide to appeal, your preparation is the same kind of preparation you'd do for any serious financial dispute: assemble the timeline, gather the notices, gather your submissions, and include your call log.

The appeal process is also where your "small, fast, hard-to-break" documentation system pays off. It's easier to request records and argue facts when you already have your own records in order.

Confidence is a system: keep a timeline that a stranger could follow

The easiest way to feel powerless is to have an unstructured pile of emails and PDFs. The easiest way to feel in control is to have a one-page timeline.

A simple timeline format:

- `2026-02-14`: Updated income estimate due to spouse leaving job.
- `2026-02-16`: Received DMI notice requesting income proof; deadline `2026-05-17`.
- `2026-02-20`: Uploaded final pay stub and employer separation letter; saved submission confirmation.
- `2026-03-05`: Called Marketplace; rep confirmed receipt, review pending.

- 2026-03-22: DMI still active; re-uploaded clearer scan with cover note.

This is not busywork. It's a way to keep the story intact when you're tired, stressed, or talking to your fifth representative.

A final practical truth: the Marketplace is easier to work with if you behave like a lender

A lender doesn't accept "trust me" as documentation. It accepts dated documents, clear amounts, and a coherent narrative. If you treat Marketplace interactions with the same seriousness—not with fear, but with professionalism—most problems shrink.

Read notices like contracts. Meet deadlines like a business owner. Save confirmations like receipts. Keep a communication log like a project manager. If something is wrong, escalate like someone who knows the rules exist for a reason.

Confidence isn't the belief that nothing will go wrong. Confidence is knowing that if something does go wrong, you can prove what happened, correct it, and keep your coverage steady without sacrificing weeks of your life to confusion.

www.ingramcontent.com/pod-product-compliance
Lightning Source LLC
LaVergne TN
LVHW010714061126
851857LV00014B/1179
* 9 7 9 8 2 5 6 2 0 3 4 2 9 *

Published by NobleTrex Press

For permissions and other inquiries, write to:

P.O. Box 3132, Framingham, MA 01701, USA

Healthcare Before Medicare

The Early Retiree's Guide to ACA Marketplace Plans, MAGI Management, and Affordable Coverage in the Gap Years

Patricia M. Ashworth